The Strange Poverty of the Rich

The Strange Poverty of the Rich

◆

Accounts of a transient artist's life

Sam Minot

iUniverse, Inc.
New York Lincoln Shanghai

The Strange Poverty of the Rich
Accounts of a transient artist's life

All Rights Reserved © 2004 by Samuel Minot

No part of this book may be reproduced or transmitted in any form or by any means, graphic, electronic, or mechanical, including photocopying, recording, taping, or by any information storage retrieval system, without the written permission of the publisher.

iUniverse, Inc.

For information address:
iUniverse, Inc.
2021 Pine Lake Road, Suite 100
Lincoln, NE 68512
www.iuniverse.com

ISBN: 0-595-31642-5 (pbk)
ISBN: 0-595-76460-6 (cloth)

Printed in the United States of America

"The fewer our wants, the closer we are to the gods."
—Socrates

Contents

Introduction		ix
CHAPTER 1	New Orleans	1
CHAPTER 2	The Seabees	12
CHAPTER 3	A migratory Life	29
CHAPTER 4	Costa Rica	69
CHAPTER 5	The Coral Route	83
CHAPTER 6	Dad's Ashes	108

Introduction

I am an artist, not much of a writer. I've lived an unusual transient lifestyle and I want to share part of my life with you. I was spending the winter of 1999–2000 in Greece, moving around the Greek Islands to paint and I finished reading the books I had brought with me. Unable to find more English books to read, I started to write my autobiography. Each night I scrawled down my memories on notebooks and I amassed enough to bring you this segment of my life.

    I was compelled to tell a true account of my life because I have three published writers in my family and they have, in a way, hijacked my life and put me into their works of fiction, often much to my dismay. Now that I am older and have settled down, I have my own computer and I've learned to type; so I was able to put this together, to publish on my. I want to get this out there so people will read it; the same way I make paintings so that people can see them. Hopefully, my messages will make it to those who have eyes that can see. You can see many of my paintings that I describe in this book on my website: www.samminot.com.

Sam Minot   4april04

1

New Orleans

When I was nineteen years old, I had a job as a plumber's helper in New Orleans. I didn't know anything about plumbing, nor did I aspire to become a plumber; I had just gotten this job at an employment office, since I was in need of work. I was paired up with different plumbers on various days, but we usually did the save things, service calls.

It was the difference in the customers that we made calls to that fascinated me so. Sometimes we would go into these small "shotguns," single story, two unit houses, in poor neighborhoods. I was appalled at the living conditions for many people crammed into these houses, perhaps seven or eight residing in a two bedroom unit. Then other times, we would approach the big houses in the Garden District, ring the bell, and wait. After a few moments of us surveying the ornate wrought-iron works and the well kept flowerbeds, someone would unlock the locks and the door would open, usually revealing an elderly man or woman looking ghostly pale. Most often they had servants as well who directed us to the plumbing problems.

In this city, the drastic differences in wealth were sometimes only a few blocks apart. Many of the mansions, with the residents who sometimes looked like the belonged in an Alfred Hitchcock film, had large walls or fences, alarm systems, closed doors and windows. Most of the ghetto houses were already open with young mothers and children playing about the stoops. Music often was blaring out of open windows. As I saw it, both groups lived a type of poverty and most likely both were born into their current living situation. At some time in the past the people on the rich side had made a fortune and I presume that all the families on the poor side had been poor, ever since they had been slaves the ancestors of the rich ones.

I myself was from Massachusetts, a Yankee, and had experienced a privileged life. One of seven children, I attended a private school in my hometown of Manchester (By-the-Sea), Massachusetts then after eighth grade I went to a prep school in Milton, Massachusetts for my high school years. After a couple years in boarding school, I became disenchanted with the path that I was taking for it seemed to funnel all of us toward an elitist way of life. It was obvious that the majority of us in school were from rich families and that many of our parents had attended private schools and theirs and so on-a superior education over that of the public schooling system, or so it is thought by the ones who have the money.

Living at boarding school, I became independent from my parents yet I was at an age where studying wasn't something that I was particularly fond of. I was more into sports and partying, a kind of juvenile delinquent who also liked to paint.

Once I completed my senior year I chose not to go to college unlike the rest of my siblings who attended such universities as Harvard, Brown, Bowdoin, Hampshire, UVM, and Barnard. I was a bit displeased and embarrassed, to a degree, as to who I was and where I came from. There was an air of arrogance within my family that I noticed in my father and in his father, so I felt it necessary that I should "cut the shoots" while I could.

So once out of school, I drove off alone to New Orleans in my little "Le Car," Dad's really, my sister had moved to New York and no longer needed it so it became available for me to use. The South was warmer in the winter and New Orleans interested me, a festive place with a history, a place I had never been to and the drinking age was still 18, where as in Massachusetts it had just gone up to 21.

No one questioned me particularly about my decision not to attend college nor did they inquire as to what I had planned to do far away in New Orleans. Our mother had died two years prior in a car accident and my father probably thought "good riddance". He and I had run into a few conflicts since my mom's death and most of his immediate concerns were with his new wife, Wendy.

I am the fifth child in this family of seven. My sister Eliza (10) was at home; Chris (16) was at prep school in Vermont; George (21) was in college in Maine; Dinah (22) lived in Somerville; Susan (23) lived with our aunt in New York City and Carrie (25) lived in New York as well, then attending Columbia business school. None of them had tabs on my radical self nor were they very close to me for we had all gone off to boarding schools as ninth graders. Once we left home we would only see each other on random weekends or holidays and perhaps in the summer when we went to an island off the coast of Maine where our family had a summer house. The fabric of a unified family that we had experienced as youngsters had dissolved, as is common in our sort of families, and was compounded due to the death of our mother.

Once there in New Orleans, I found an apartment and I decided to learn how to weld, so I could get myself a job in one of the many shipyards in the area. I went to a school, Airco Tech, for six months which my dad gladly paid for. Upon completion, I was employed temporarily at a shipyard in New Orleans East for I was promptly laid off. It was the early eighties and Reaganomics was kicking in, lots of layoffs in the Steel Industries. That is when I had to get a different job which was as the plumber's helper.

I am an artist as well, a painter mostly. I had a natural love for drawing and painting ever since I was a child. I always got an "A" in art class at high school and I even won an award, The Wigglesworth Art Prize, my senior year. At this time in New Orleans I was doing mostly abstracts, paintings that looked fractured and all broken up, but colorful and vibrant. I painted on weekends mostly. I also explored the neighborhoods, found marijuana to smoke, and I drank a lot!

I took the bus early each morning across town to Al Bourgeois Plumbing and Heating. I was one of the only white people on the bus that went down Louisiana Avenue, through the Magnolia Housing Projects and ended at Canal St. where I walked the rest of the way to where I worked. After work I took the same bus home, cooked my own meals, drank some beers, and watched my little black and white TV. Often on weekends I wandered over to a club nearby, Tipitina's, where I listened to great music that played. One could just sit on the sidewalk outside the club and easily hear the bands that played inside.

I slowly met people who lived in the neighborhood near there. Once I got drunk enough, I went over across the street to a bar, The Rose Tattoo, where only black people were.

I was fond of black women for three years earlier I had experienced my first romance with a black girl when I spent a summer in the West Indies on the island: St. Eustatius or "Statia," as it was more commonly called. I went there on a work program called "Crossroads Africa". Her name was Laurel, nicknamed Latchi, and she was my first love, a beautiful girl the same age I was but physically more mature. She came up to our hut where the five of us and our adult group leader stayed. I liked her and when she one day, while playing cards, put her barefoot on mine under the table and smiled at me, I fell in love with her! We spent time together down at the beach looking for blue glass slave beads in the sand near an old fort. We swam together and chased each other along the beach. I was impressed that she could run faster than I could! At the town dances, we danced in the local style of a kind of hip grinding close dance to the reggae and calypso music. We kissed while sitting together alone.

I left Statia with my group, and when flying away on our little plane, I remember circling and looking down on that little island, saddened, knowing that I would never see her again. My yearning for a similar experience stayed with me for years to come.

It wasn't all that long until I found myself a girlfriend in New Orleans. She was Manya, a short, thin black woman I had met at the Rose Tattoo. She came over to my apartment at times and brought some of her friends too.

I was pretty bold about integrating and especially once I got drunk, I was fearless or clueless really as to where I went at night. I went along with her and her friends into these small bars and clubs that didn't have one other white person in them. At times I caught grief for being a type of racial intruder, I guess, but they would stick up for me or we would leave. I had a car—none of them did, so we often drove off to some late night breakfast or we just cruised and parked at different places like at the levy or at the lakefront.

Each of the girls I met was around my age or little older and they already had kids. They were single moms and many of them collected welfare and many of them lived with their mothers. When they went out at night their moms would watch their kids. This was very different from my peers back home in New England where practically no one past 18 still lived with their parents. Most everyone went off to college and after that they often had high paying jobs right from the start. Many who married and had kids could purchase their own homes and independently raise their children, often having a live-in nanny to help out if they were wealthy enough to afford it.

In these ghettos of New Orleans, I noticed some admirable qualities amidst the poverty. Maybe it was crowded in these little houses but there were a lot of hands to help, many other children to play with, and always other relatives or neighbors to watch over each others' children. I liked this big family atmosphere but I was an outsider. I wanted to be like them and I tended to blindly befriend others that I met in their neighborhoods. Some warned me of others, that I might get hurt. I was completely ignorant of the violence that occurred in these streets and I soon gathered that most of the guys had spent at least some time in prison. One fellow informed me that going to prison was nothing-all his friends were in there and he could get good drugs and meals were free! In the status of freedom, he was unemployed and hustled to make a living.

I was taken to the jail, Central Lockup, once. It was a Friday evening and I was downtown with these two other guys looking to buy some drugs. We were on the edge of the Iberville Housing Project where I waited out on the sidewalk while they went in to make a score. Since I'm a white person, I stayed behind, being too conspicuous if I went in there too. The guy I knew better, Dynell, handed me this long fishing knife before they left me alone. I said that I didn't need it but he said that he felt better if I had something to protect myself in case I was jumped; so I put it in my pocket, sat down on a wall and waited for them to return. In about twenty minutes they did return but had failed to get anything. Suddenly a police car skidded to a halt in front of us. The other guy with us bolted as soon as they stopped but Dynell and I were apprehended and arrested.

"I wouldn't want to have this thing in my stomach!" said the police officer sitting in the passenger seat, testing the sharp point of the long knife he had found in my pocket.

They took us both in, charging me with carrying a concealed weapon and Dynell with obstructing the sidewalk, since he had nothing illegal on him. We were put into a cell that had four bunk beds and we had to wait until Tuesday to go to court for it was a long weekend due to a holiday. The cell filled up quickly and over the next few days there were a few fights. We kept together and fended off troublemakers. Tuesday morning we were all herded into court, handcuffed together in a human chain. I was set free on my own recognizance. I had to return to municipal court three months down the road, charged with carrying a concealed weapon (the knife was over six inches), a felony that carried a three month sentence. That frightened me for just a few days in jail were most unpleasant.

I kept working my job with the plumber and they put me on a sewer detail with this 70-year-old man, Ken. The owner of the company, Al, brought me into his office one day and asked me if I minded working with Ken, an old black man. I replied that it was fine and he said to me, "Where you from boy?" I told him. He knew I was a Yankee. He told me that this man Ken was a preacher. "Can you imagine that!" he said slapping his knee with surprise. Ken spoke a hard to comprehend broken English that was common in the South amongst the poor, both black and white. I had already encountered this with various people I had met and I thought it to be cool to have learned how to follow their talk. I even began to adopt it in my own speech, even more so when I got drunk, to assimilate amongst them.

"Let me learn ya somethin Sam!" Ken would say to me as he pushed his sharp shooter shovel with his foot into the dirt, followed by a big spit of tobacco juice. He chewed cigars, opening one from its cellophane wrapper and chomping half of it into his mouth. Our job was to located broken sewer lines and to dig down to them. If they were terracotta pipes we could replace them. To cut the pipes he used a hatchet, hitting and turning then until they cracked. If the pipes were cast iron some other guys came and finished the job. I was shocked to learn that Ken earned the same wage per hour that I did, $5.00.

One day on the job we were carrying a heavy duty router cable machine, or "snake" as they called it, in the back of our pick-up truck. Not being secured properly, it rolled out off the bed of the truck and fell onto the street while we were at a stop sign. Neither of us noticed this until a car behind us kept honking their horn; even so, we didn't look back right away for I think that we both feared it was some racist person honking at us. Finally, Ken noticed in his rear view mirror what had happened, for our machine was being carried across the neutral ground or median by two young men. Stealing our machine, they loaded it into the back of their van and drove off in the other direction. The boss wasn't too happy but theft was an all too common occurrence in this city. It made the racist whites more justified in their narrow minded racist views.

Racism happened on both sides yet I noticed that most people I met there weren't prejudice. Both races had been living together for three or four hundred years there and there was a great deal of mixed blood, known there as Creoles. Many of the people there deemed black looked pretty white to me. Mayor Dutch Morial was an African-American but he looked paler than my father was. It was a far more segregated society back where I came from in Massachusetts. Of course we in my family didn't consider ourselves racists but none of us knew anyone other than other white people in our homogeneous society. It was mostly through music and musicians like Stevie Wonder, Al Green, and Aretha Franklin that we were exposed to the African-American culture in America.

My date came up to go to court from when I was arrested and my father had kindly set me up with a lawyer whom I had talked to on the phone. He told me what he looked like and what he would be wearing so that I could find him when I went to court. My brother George came down to New Orleans during his Spring break and he came to court with me. I took the morning off from work and we arrived at the courthouse about a half hour before the day's sessions got underway, as my lawyer had instructed me to. Once there, I found my lawyer and we talked a bit about the case. He told me that since I had no previous offences he could probably get it down to thirty days. That was still a frightful thought to me. My lawyer asked me if I saw in the courtroom the policeman who had arrested us. I didn't see him. He wasn't there yet. My lawyer then went up and had a conference with the judge. A few moments later the court assembled and the show got under way. My name was called off first! The lawyer had made this happen. Since the arresting officer was absent, the case was dismissed. My lawyer smartly shook my hand, snapped shut his briefcase and told me that I was free to go. George and I looked at each other with amazement and we exited the building. As we were leaving, the officer who had arrested me walked right by us, just a little late, thankfully.

The hot months of summer came along and I became lazy. I quit my job without thoroughly understanding the consequences, no cash flow. After paying my rent, I had little money left. Uninspired to look for another job, I stayed in my apartment, painted abstract paintings and drank a lot. I spent the remnants of my earnings on cigarettes and beer. I bought large bags of red kidney beans and rice that I could subsist on for weeks. Now I was in the same boat as many of my new found friends-I was falling into poverty. It was miserably hot and humid and soon enough my food was gone. I called my dad up asking him for some money, making up a story that I needed to pay a dentist bill. I waited for his $300. check to arrive in the mail. I fasted, hungry and destitute but unfazed for I wanted to experience what it was like to be poor, to be even poorer than the others.

I had visitors come over and they treated me to some malt liquor or marijuana they brought along. They saw how I didn't have any food or anything and some suggested that I at least sell my car. I couldn't for it was owned by my dad; but I didn't tell them that.

A new guy moved into the apartment next to mine. His name was Terry, a balding man in his early forties. He said he was a Vietnam veteran and he was also a drug addict who shot drugs. He had a bottled solution of opium and morphine that he said he got from a doctor in San Francisco. I wanted to try it and he showed me how to find a vein to shoot into. I liked the instantaneous results of injecting drugs but I was very cautious of their dangers as well. I tried other drugs he got like heroin and coke and other pharmaceuticals that I didn't even know the names of.

Fortunately this stint of shooting drugs didn't last all that long. One morning I heard a crashing next door at Terry's and an argument and fight ensued. I didn't want to get involved so I went down my back staircase on the other side of the house only to be intercepted by a man and two women. I recognized one of the women, she was a druggie friend of Terry's and she said to me, "You're not going anywhere!" Shortly two men came around the corner. One was this white trash girl's boyfriend and the other was a heavy set guy who carried a chain that he had just used on Terry. I stood still a ways up on the staircase, ready to leap over the railing to run.

"We're not going to hurt you," the man with chain said. "Terry stole shit from me!" I paused without saying anything and they all climbed into their car parked right there and they drove off.

I walked back up into my apartment and phoned the police, telling them that a man was attacked in my building, then I went over to Terry's and found him hunched over his kitchen sink washing blood off his face which was bloated and black and blue already.

"Did you get them?" he asked me.

"No, they left. I called the police though."

"Oh, that's just great!" he said angrily. "Why didn't you get them? Don't you have a baseball bat or something?"

"That guy said you stole stuff from him." He didn't respond and continued to wash his face for blood was streaming out of his forehead.

The police arrived in about fifteen minutes and Terry told them that he had been burglarized, adding that his neighbor, me, didn't come to his aid. I didn't say anything but one of the officers said, "Yeah, sometimes you don't know who your friends are!"

They took him to the hospital and Terry soon moved out or was evicted. This experience shook me up, making me re-assess my life and the direction I was taking. I had the wrong kind of friends and I was now a drug addict too. I wanted to change my life but I didn't know how. I was so far away from home and I was totally alone, suffering from withdrawals because I had no drugs and from hunger because I had no money to buy food.

Forced by hunger, I went out and found myself a new job—it was on the West Bank in Westwego—a construction plumbing job. They were building these duplex houses and I helped the plumbers with the copper water lines and the PVC stacking for waste and venting. The job didn't last very long, about five weeks; then I was laid off. I earned some money but before it was time to pay my rent I left an unsigned money order in my apartment and a visiting girl stole it from me. I called my dad to again ask for some money and he was furious with me. He said that he wasn't going to send me any more money. I told him I was coming home.

"You can't stay here!" he told me.

"Why not?" I asked him.

"Wendy (his wife) doesn't want you to." He told me to drive to Norfolk, Virginia and to join the Navy. Our conversation ended. The Navy! Forget it. What a drag that would be!

Consequently, I did wind up enlisting into the Navy. I had nowhere to stay and I only had enough money to make it in a drive back to Massachusetts. I called my dad again on the drive back north, informing him that one is unable to just walk up and enlist into the military, perhaps the way it was in his day. He agreed that I could stay with them if I enlisted as soon as I got home. I really had no options so I did it, joining at the local recruiting station in Salem, Ma. My recruiter signed me up for a five year hitch with the Seabees, misinforming me that it was the minimum enlistment. I didn't know what the Seabees were but I had construction experience with welding and plumbing so I thought I would be doing more of that only I signed up as an EO (equipment operator) which meant operating heavy equipment, no welding or plumbing-these were separate ratings in the Seabees. I really was completely ignorant of what I was getting into. I was in a delayed entry program and I had to wait six months before I went off to boot camp.

My dad promptly set me up with a job through a client of his at his bank. It was as a laborer in a lumberyard that was quite far away, about an hour's drive. I mostly just walked around and picked up trash, metal bands, paper and broken pieces of lumber that accumulated in the yard or I assisted the forklift operators make up their orders. It was a boring job and at $5 an hour I only fetched, after taxes, $130 a week. But, I wasn't complaining, for I had experienced the hardships of being hungry and destitute prior to that.

By chance one Friday after work I took a different route home, driving through Boston and into Revere where I drove by Suffolk Downs. I went in, totally naïve as to what occurred in there, thinking maybe it was a car race track or something. It wasn't. It was a horse track where gambling on thoroughbreds was the activity. Ignorant of how to play, I asked another handicapper there how to place bets. At first I lost a few dollars then I noticed that there was the trifecta, a bet that chooses for three horses to finish in exact order. I bought a single trifecta ticket for $3 and miraculously, I won! Winning a whopping $1,200., I was amazed at my own beginner's luck. I took my winnings and left.

I stayed in Boston that evening and explored the Combat Zone, the seedy part of town that had strip clubs and prostitutes. I did want to find a woman to have sex with but doing it this way was a bit embarrassing. I went into some clubs where they had topless girls dancing and very expensive drinks. I tried other bars, not really liking what I saw; however, in one place, one woman caught my instant attention. I thought she was beautiful! Dressed in red, she had very dark skin, straightened hair and Chinese-like eyes set wide apart behind her rounded glasses. She certainly didn't look like a prostitute, a whore, to me; in fact, I thought she might even be an undercover policewoman or something to that effect. She noticed me looking at her and she came over and sat next to me.

"Want a date?" she asked me.

"Yes I do. Do you cost money?" I said and she laughed. "Well how much does this cost then?"

"Well it's 100 for a suck and a fuck," she said softly and closely into my ear; then she smiled at me, her white teeth gleaming on her dark face in the darkened room. I agreed and we went out to my car. She instructed me as to where to drive to, a place she used to take her tricks to.

We drove down Huntington Avenue to a place she used. She told me her name was Katina and she asked me things about myself. She soon told me where to park, in front of a brownstone near Northeastern University. We went inside to a foyer where she was buzzed in from downstairs; then we walked upstairs where she knocked on a door. An old woman opened the door and checked me out from head to tow for a second, then she let us in. It was sort of a "cat house" where some ladies of the night plied their trade.

We went into a private bedroom and Katina asked me to pay her first. I paid her what she asked for then we had sex. I thought she was beautiful—sleek figured yet strong boned with soft dark skin that felt cooler than mine. After I took off my clothes she told me that I was cute and she giggled a little to herself. She gave me some head then we had intercourse in a sitting position, both of us facing each other. I tried to kiss her but she rejected that, telling me that she doesn't kiss her clients.

Once done I drove her back to the place I found her in the Combat Zone and told her that I wanted to see her again. She said that she usually came in on Friday and Saturday nights. I drove all the way back home with thoughts of the strange, seemingly lucky day that I had, poking into the shady events of gambling and prostitution. I knew these things to be sort of sins, but I had been sort of blessed with a windfall of profits from betting and a wonderful sexual encounter with this beautiful woman. I was completely unaware that I had entered a type of trap that would cause me to suffer in future.

I did my job at the lumberyard all week and the next Friday after work I stayed in Boston again to meet up with that same girl. Sure enough, she was there again and we went out and did the same thing. This time she was a bit more open, telling me that she was from Sharon but now lived in Roxbury, that she had a little daughter, and that she formerly had been a third grade school teacher.

This time when we had sex she asked me if I liked to eat pussy. I said that I did but she could tell that I was a neophyte once I started on her, so she gave me accurate instructions on what to do to please a woman. She then gave me oral sex with no instructions on my part.

All week at work I thought about this woman. Regularly, I visited her, giving her most all of the money that I earned. I started frequenting the track more often to multiply my small paycheck, but most often, I lost more than I won. When I did lose all my money she was reluctant to go out with me, telling me that she had to earn money for her baby. I was driving myself crazy for I felt that I was in love with her and I told her this. She was seven years older than I was and didn't take me very seriously, adding that she had taken a vow to herself not to get serious with any of her clients. When we talked about love she said, "When you love someone, you don't expect something in return." I understood this wisdom but I didn't experience it. I wanted a reciprocating love her. I felt that she really liked me, but she always left me up in the air as to who I was to her. I was jealous that she had sex with other men and I worried for her safety for some bad person might assault her. If I gave her enough money she went home and didn't go back to that seedy bar. She said her free choice to be a prostitute was only temporary and that it was just a fast way to make a lot of money to support her child.

Later in the year, I learned that she lived with another woman who also hustled. Since I had become this track hound she and her friend came with me once to the dog track. I won a little then we all went to a hotel and had sex. Once there, they started kissing each other! I was surprised that they were lovers.

In the ensuing months I continued my bad habits of drinking and gambling. I felt terrible at times, having worked all week and then losing it all in an hour or less at the race track. I started taking things from our house, stealing them to sell to get more money which I brought back to gamble at the track. We had inconspicuous bags of old silver trays, flatware, and things from my dad's ancestors stored down in a room deep in the cellar. There was still an ancient light bulb that worked in that cave-like room. I knew that what I was doing was wrong; but I did it spitefully, for I felt that my father had unfairly sanctioned money from me that my older siblings had received from our grandmother.

The degenerative life that I was leading soon came to an end, for a while anyway, for my date to go into the Navy had arrived. It was Halloween and I was flown to San Diego where a bunch of us recruits were met by Navy personnel who shuttled us in vans to the Recruit Training Center.

2

The Seabees

Basic training, or boot camp, as it is called, really sucked. They started yelling at us in the van on the way to the base. It was very stressful for these Nazi types would get seriously angry at you. We got our heads shaved, very little sleep, horrid food and insidious duties. Hours are spent on instructions about how to fold our clothes, to make our beds, and to polish our shoes and belt buckles. This is accompanied by lots of push ups, sit ups and jumping jacks. After a few days, one is put into a company that you stay with for the duration of boot camp, which is eight weeks.

Each company is around eighty guys. I was in a drill company which supposedly contained the smarty guys with the higher ASVAB test scores; plus, we had the musicians, for eventually we were to do the ceremonies for the graduating companies and other festive events. We also had the fifty state flags that fifty of us would carry and learn how to handle, raising and lowering them in sync in a sort of wave. I carried Indiana's state flag!

We all did everything together. We looked similar with our bald heads and the same clothes and we all had to march everywhere together. As simple as it sounds, it takes quite some time before a group of eighty can march in unison. We moved around the perimeters of the open asphalt lots, known as grinders, and when we had to turn at a right angle one side of the walking rectangle had to slow down while the opposite side fanned around in bigger steps to catch up with the row they were in. There were commands to make turns, flanks, and about faces, and the Company Commander could order us to halt at anytime. We had to freeze and if anyone was not in a perfect row, everyone paid with push-ups. We marched to the mess hall and to other buildings to take classes about Navy stuff. If you got tired in class you couldn't doze off so you would stand up in the rear of the classroom. Never could you just go walking off on your own, unless you had a walking chit, a special note that gave you permission to do so.

There was no escape from the group. All eighty of us slept side by side on cots in one big room. If one person failed in their inspection all of us paid for it. It was kind of a primal experience for it attempted to extinguish the individual, to mold him into a part of the whole group. The military is about following orders from above without questioning them. It was pertinent for each person to follow "the chain of command," the hierarchy of the military, where someone in a higher rank dictates all orders to his subordinates. The whole experience of basic training was a drag, but they all assured us that it was the worst part of joining the Navy.

Finally, at the end of boot camp, we got liberty, meaning that we could go off the base. The rules were that we had to where our dress whites, no civilian clothes, and that we weren't to go to Tijuana. They let us out in our sailor's cap and dress whites. I went off on my own to a store and I bought some civilian clothes to wear, rented a hotel room then took a train to Tijuana, Mexico where I went, like magnet, to a horse track there, and started drinking beer. I hadn't had any alcohol for over two months; probably the longest stint I had been sober since I had started drinking in the sixth grade! I came back to San Diego on the train and I started to look for a woman.

I wandered around in the city looking for a bar or nightclub to go to. I was impressed by the cleanliness of this city, compared to other cities I had seen back East. I passed a place that was quite full, overflowing out onto the sidewalk, only nothing there enticed me to go in. Country western music played, muffled by the voices of the garrulous bunch inside. I saw through a large window a bunch of fleet tweets dressed in their dress whites, standing in a row, looking like human bowling pins lined up next to the bar.

Further along, I found a club to enter. Music I knew from New Orleans, Cameo, was playing inside, so I went in. It was more what I was looking for. There were mostly black women inside. I sat down and ordered a beer. Instantly, a girl sat next to me and asked me if I would buy her a drink. I did, but I didn't find her very attractive. I kept watching the dancers and didn't talk to her so after a while she left. Another woman approached me who was more attractive. She asked me to dance and we did. We sat back down and she told me her name was Barbara and that for $50 we could go back to her place and fuck. I agreed and followed her outside where we grabbed a cab to a hotel room she had not far away.

Once there we had sex. She was stacked, with curves that gave me an erection instantly! I was really plastered from drinking all afternoon but I had a type of adrenaline surge that kept me going for a long time. I was wearing a condom and

I felt it rip as the head of my cock grew inside her. She felt this but urged me to continue.

I woke up in the morning disoriented and hung over. I noticed I was alone and that my clothes were gone! She had taken everything of mine, including my wallet with my military I D. We had been warned since day one that losing your military I D was a big "no, no," an automatic "short tour," a series of grueling exercises that last for four hours! Only my black chloroform shoes remained there on the floor, unwanted by just about anybody. I walked out to the reception office garbed in a white bed sheet, telling the person there what had happened. They called the police.

I went back to my room, her room, and waited for the police to arrive. They showed up and chuckled at me wrapped in a sheet, like a toga. I embarrassingly told them my story, just another common occurrence in this navy town to them. One officer knew who Barbara was and he questioned my judgment about the night before. I told them that I had a hotel room of my own at another hotel and they brought me over there where I dressed back into my dress whites. The cops even gave me a ride in their cruiser back to the base for I had no money to pay for a cab. The sentries at the gate saw me get out of the police cruiser and after I told them that my ID had been stolen, they gave me a nod to enter back into the base to report to my company. Once there, I had to tell the CC (Company Commander) that my I D had been stolen. He affirmed that I was headed for a "short tour".

A dozen or so of us naughty recruits reported to this unpleasant event at 8 am the next morning. The term "short tour" was left over from the old days when they would have to carry buckets of sand, on the run, back and forth across the base. The ones today were different.

We all stood in squares marked in white about one yard wide. Each of us had a mock M1 riffle, which throughout basic training, we had learned to handle with various moves. We had to hold the rifle with both hands when we did push-ups, sit ups, and jumping jacks.

Two short Phillipinos fellows were in charge and they explained the rules. Each of us was allowed only twelve hits, meaning that anything you did wrong was a hit counted against you. Lots of things can be hits: if you failed to complete the exercise ordered; if you couldn't utter the count while exercising; if you, when asked, were unable to state a particular person in the chain of command; if you didn't know the "word of the day," which changed every day. All this stuff and more were at hand for the four hours of exercising, with five minute breaks every half hour. I was in pretty good shape and had been through comparable physical training in all the sports I had played in high school, soccer, hockey and lacrosse. This "short tour" was difficult but I completed it as did two other guys. The rest who failed it had to start basic training all over again at day one.

I finished boot camp and was given orders for public works at Guantanamo Bay, Cuba. First, I had to go the EO school which was for two months in Gulfport, Ms. This school turned out to be even worse than boot camp! We had a crazy CC who at one moment would be laughing and joking and the next be irate, working himself into a fervor over anything, as though he was completely insane. No matter how clean or well kept things were, it was never good enough. All this was the same head game as at boot camp. We had to do lots of exercising and one time we all stood at attention for six hours straight! Some guys keeled over, hitting the floor with a crunching thud. The CC often made crude jokes while we stood at attention. "I was eating this woman's pussy and I found some corn kernels up there inside her." If someone laughed he blew up at them. "Did I say you could laugh!" he screamed. "I'm gonna tear your head off and shit in the hole!"

The training we did there was simply to familiarize ourselves with the heavy equipment machinery that we would later be operating. We practiced operating graders, dozers, scrapers, rough terrain forklifts and more. We all lived in one big room, bunks and lockers side by side, and we weren't allowed much free time. When I could, I walked over to get drunk at the bowling alley or at a bar off base. I finally finished this training school then I flew down to Guantanamo Bay, Cuba where I had my new job.

I hadn't known anything about this base, known endearingly as Gitmo, a nine-mile piece of real estate in the southeast corner of the island. Somehow, due to some old contract, the US had kept this land after their revolution. I heard a check was sent to Castro each year to pay for this forced lease, but he never even cashed them. We used the base now for fleet training operations for the navy ships in the Caribbean. It was surrounded by active minefields, ours and theirs. Castro had cut off the fresh water supply from the island, so we had a desalination plant that made fresh water and supplied the base with electricity, an expensive undertaking. The whole base seemed to be quite a waste of taxpayers' money. It was a little American town with a school and housing units for the six thousand people who lived and worked there. I was to be there for one year working as a Seabee in public works which involved the maintenance of the base. I was twenty-two years old and back in the sunny West Indies.

We Seabees wore greens, high boots and a starched hat, unlike the sailor's cap, blue shirt and dungarees that the sailors wore, or "fleet tweets" as they were derogatorily deemed by the Seabees. I never even went on a ship. The emblem on our shirt was of a cartoon-like bumblebee that held in its hands a hammer, a wrench, and a machine gun! We had to do a little combat training twice a year with the marines, known as DEFEX or defense exercises. I never was very fond of guns and things, but we all had to throw hand grenades, launch off a single shot of an expensive one-timer bazooka known as a LAW rocket, and fire the incredibly powerful 50 cal which made big splashes in the water two or three miles away, across an inlet in the bay where dummy rusted trucks were sunken into sandbanks as target practice. Our job as Seabees was in construction. The other rates were the builders, steelworkers, engineer aides, and the mechanics. The mechanics worked with us EOs in Alpha Company.

I first worked in the motor pool where all the vehicles and construction equipment were kept. It was a like a big rent-all place there, only everything was signed out free of charge. People came to get things from rakes and shovels, chainsaws and packers, to cars and busses. Even dump trucks and mobile cranes were kept in this yard. I worked with Petty Officer Beddows in a little hut in the center of the yard. It was often quiet and boring after items were checked in the mornings. I even dozed off sitting on the couch next to his desk. As long as I popped up when a customer came, Beddows didn't mind. "You're like a cat!" He remarked at my ability to sleep and to then awake, wary of visitors who approached the hut. He was a good man, Beddows, the type who played the military game without true sincerity for he was married with two kids and needed the higher paycheck of the upper ranking enlisted man.

He and I went out fishing on some weekends. There wasn't much to do at Gitmo, but the Caribbean Sea was rich with sea life, making excellent snorkeling and fishing. We would rent, at minimum charge, these pontoon boats that had outboard motors and at dusk we would go out to the mouth of the river and anchor there to fish all night. Dolphins often frolicked playfully around the boat at sunset on their way out to the open ocean. Once it became dark we lit a lantern and hung it on the side of the boat to attract lots of little fish which attracted lots of bigger fish. Most everyone used squid for bait, but I showed him another way to fish by snagging live bait. Using a sole treble hook, I cast over a school of fish, let it sink a bit, then I jerked my rod back to snag a single fish. In a matter of seconds, when the other ones scatter, mine is an easy meal. I figured this technique out one summer in Maine when the bluefish were running.

We caught all sorts of fish. Amberjacks put up great fights and were good eating too. Red snapper and grouper, barracuda and king mackerel were also caught. Sometimes fish jumped into the boat in the melee that occurred around the boat due to the lantern attracting the denizens of the deep; or suddenly, all the fish disappeared and a menacing shark cruised alongside our pontoon boat. We hauled in too much fish really, but it all went to good use for we ate some ourselves and sold the rest for pennies a pound to the Jamaicans who lived on the base. There was a little village on top of a hill in the town where they all stayed, about two thousand of them. I later worked on a paving crew and got to know some of them.

I held mostly mundane jobs at Gitmo, working at a rock crusher then at a cement batching plant. At the rock crusher we loaded up dump trucks with large rocks then backed them into an elevated spot above the rock crushing apparatus where the rocks were dumped down into a square metal box that funneled into the powerful, crunching jaws that broke the rocks up. The newly broken rocks fell through screens that could be changed to determine the size of the rocks desired. Conveyor belts moved the gravel up ramps where they fell off at their ends into a freefall where they mounted into neat conical piles. Often my duty at this rock crusher was to just stand there on the gizmo, which vibrated tremendously, and watch so that I could turn it off if large metal scraps or logs fell into the jaws.

The cement plant wasn't as uncomfortable but it was boring. Two of us manned this station that was a drive through for the TMs or transit mixers. They pulled in below these large cisterns that held the sand and gravel which we emptied into their holding tanks; then we broke open bags of cement and poured them in as well for whatever desired mix of concrete was appropriated. It was hot and dusty out there, but it wasn't a strenuous job for often we just waited out there for the TMs to come back and fill up. More than once I had to climb into a TM's tank and jackhammer out concrete that had hardened up due to some operator's neglect.

We all rotated around in our jobs, but the lower one is in rank, the more unskilled and menial was the job. On the asphalt crews, I worked with a rake and a shovel, the same as the Jamaican laborers. Public works was like a nine to five job. I earned $250 every two weeks and my checks mounted in my savings for I had no bills to pay. I only spent money on cigarettes and beer which were cheap there on the base.

I lived in the barracks, a dorm-like place with two bunks per room. It was crowded living but I could cope for I had already lived in a similar situation back at boarding school. For many of the guys, it was their first time away from home. If one was married, special housing units were available on the base. Also, in the military, one got paid more for each child that they had as dependants. It was easy to see why many with kids were geared for the long twenty year hitch for at thirty eight they could get a pension and receive all the medical benefits for life. In the common room area of the barracks was a television that receive the AFRTS (armed forces radio and television service) and a Cuban station that played nationalist propaganda as well as some sporting events. We had a coke machine that dispensed canned beers for a quarter, four of the five choices were for beer. One was for coke.

The Seabees were renowned for their "can do," work hard, play hard attitude. They were famous for trashing bars in foreign countries during drunken rampages. Many of the guys were your biker type, white guys who liked heavy metal music, listening to the likes of ACDC or Quiet Riot. At times there were fights in the barracks and onlookers jeered support for their victor while the two guys slugged out their dispute.

Once early in my stay, I was in a type of fight with this guy who lived a couple doors down the hall. Both drunk, we were talking one evening about things and I mentioned that my mother had died. As he nodded his head in a solemn way, I misunderstood his mannerisms and asked him if his mother had died as well. This uncorked him and he wanted to beat me up! I tried to calm him down for I didn't want to fight. Unsuccessful, I left his room. Making it back to my room, I shut the door. In a rage, the guy kept pounding on our door so I opened it and he took a swing at me. I dodged his pot shot and his fist smacked into the door jam, furthering his fury. "Look, I don't want to hurt you," I told him, not that I would for he was about fifty pounds heavier than I.

"You don't want to hurt me!" he said in a rage that reddened his normally pale face. He swung at me again, connecting this time with the side of my face, sending me back into the room. My roommates shut the door and locked it, meanwhile this guy kept pounding on his fists against the metal door. After a few moments, the watch got the shore patrol and they subdued him in the hallway.

The next day this belligerent fellow was most amicable in his sober state and he serenely apologized to me. He inspected my face and was most stunned for he hadn't left any mark. "Normally when I hit someone like I hit you there's a shiner or a busted nose or something!" He kept searching my face. Others there were impressed at the hardness of my head as well, for they had heard the loud concussion of his fist to the side of my face. This man never bothered me again.

The months went by and I became unhappy with my life in the military, especially with the outlook that I had four years to go in my enlistment. I reflected on how it had been my financial scene and a couple unfortunate events that had landed me in the navy. It was that stolen money order and the failure to cover my rent back in New Orleans that had led me to where I now was. Had I played my cards like my other brothers and sisters, I would have been in college with spending money! The older siblings had received some stocks from Grandma's estate which Daddy withheld from me due to my insolent nature. I knew that my life and my ideals were a bit different than my siblings for I was, to a degree, ashamed of my heritage. I identified more with my mother's egalitarian, Irish Catholic side. How many of my classmates in Prep School had wound up in the military? None! If anyone from that school had gone into the military, I guarantee that it was the officer route after college. I learned quite a bit more about the officer world in the upcoming year, adding to my already congealed ideas about the poverty of the rich.

We were allowed a week of R&R after six months on Cuba. A bunch of us went to Jamaica on a small plane, all free of charge. There were two destinations: Montego Bay and Kingston. I chose to go to Kingston, wanting to see the more dangerous "Trenchtown" that Bob Marley had sung about.

Once there I went off on my own again. In the parking lot at the airport there were hoards of men trying to make a buck by selling trinkets and wooden carvings. Others offered rides in their self-anointed taxi cabs. I chose a hefty guy that looked trustworthy. I told him how I had just come from Gitmo and that I wanted to find a place to stay in town for a few days. "I can help ya out, mon. I know just the place for ya!" he told me. "We'll find some women that want to meet ya too. Are ya alone? Where's yer buddies?"

"Yes, I'm alone. I prefer it this way."

"I admire that. This can be a mighty dangerous place." He held out his hand and introduced himself as Frank. I looked into his eyes and saw trusting look on his face.

"I'm Sam." I told him. I got in his large tan sedan and we drove off. In the car, I told him how I liked reggae music and ganja too. He told me it was easy to get some and he stopped at a little store where I purchased an ounce for $10.! "I'll never smoke all this in the next few days," I admitted to him.

"That's okay mon, you can give the rest of it to me when ya go!" he said smiling. We drove on through the shanty villages of Kingston to an area known as Spanish Town where his friend had a place with rooms to rent. I noticed, on many street corners, uniformed policemen carrying M16s like the kind we practiced with. It was obvious that there was a great deal of violence in these city streets. "It's my home," Frank told me. "I've lived in Florida too, but I love it here the most." We arrived at his friend's and went in. "Oh Sam!" he hollered into the house. A middle aged Latina woman greeted us at the metal gate door to their house. She unlocked it and we went in where I met the other Sam there.

"For name's sake Sam!" said the elderly black fellow. I told him that my last name was Minot and they laughed. "We've got lots of Minotts in this neighborhood now!" I knew it was a common name there in Jamaica, due to the remnants of the British Colonialists. I also knew of the Jamaican Reggae star, Sugar Minott. Sam showed me some rooms that he had to rent and I took one. Frank said that he would come back later, if I was interested, to give a further tour of the island. I agreed and asked him how much he charged.

"We'll work somethin out, mon!" He patted me on the back. I was so stoned from not having smoked any marijuana for months. It was like I was tripping! I passed out in my room.

The next morning I had a little breakfast cooked up by Sam's wife. It was spicy fish and onions served with strong black coffee. It was Saturday morning and Sam had a couple of friends over. They were examining the racing form to place bets on the day's horse races.

"You a handicapper Sam?" he asked me. I, almost embarrassed, admitted that I was. "Well I can place a bet for you if you like!" he pushed the racing form over my way. "This here is one I like #5 and this is our best jockey on that one #8."

"Alright, I'll try $20 to win on this #8." I gave him the money to later place a bet for me. Frank came back and told me that he had to make a drive up to Ocho Rios and he offered for me to come along if I liked. I went with him in his car and we took the long drive that seemed to continually go uphill slightly into denser forests and taller trees. We went by a red lake, colored so because of the soil's pigment, through little towns that lined the meandering road's edge, past women who walked barefoot and wore sort of turbans on their heads that held in their drying curlers. "Wow!" I said as I noticed a beautiful girl wave at the two of us in his car.

"Ya see that mon!" Frank said to me with a little chuckle. Ocho Rios was beautiful but it was built up a little more with fancy hotels for the tourists. He took care of some business there and we drove back to Spanish Town. On a street corner there we saw two young white guys looking a little despondent. "Do you know them mon?" Frank asked me. Incredibly I did! They were two other guys who were on the plane from Gitmo. He stopped and we picked them up. They both were quite young, about eighteen, and their trip hadn't gone very well so far for they had been robbed. They came back and stayed where I was at Sam's place.

That night Frank took us to an outdoor dance where each of us found girls to bring back to our rooms. There were many girls at the dance and several would come up to you to ask you to dance with them. I danced with a couple of these island girls then found one that I liked and she came back and slept with me.

Our R&R weekend was soon over and Frank took us all back to the airport He was glad to have made a little profit from the three of us. We zoomed back in style to Cuba in the little eight-seater airplane only to rejoin our mundane, prison-like life at the base. Other guys had gone to Montego Bay and everybody got laid. Many liked talking about their first time with black women. My roommate said, "I was looking down at her while I was fucking her and all I could see in the dark was her white teeth."

The next job I had at Gitmo was as the CO's (Commanding Officer) chauffeur. I was picked out of my company to be the captain's driver. I didn't really want to do it, but one doesn't have a choice and I was told that it was an easy job with lots of free time. My duties were to keep the car, a black and white sedan, clean and to obviously drive the CO around the base. In the mornings, I reported to his office where his secretary, Laura, told me if there was any driving needed that day. Mostly, I just sat at a desk next to Laura's and I did pencil drawings or read until I was dismissed. One drawing I did was a detailed account of an urban scene that looked the way it might after a huge bomb had hit. Skeletal frames of broken buildings still stood amongst debris that covered the street. Laura was impressed with my artistic talent, but she cringed at the subject matter. It was me really, analogous to my life. It had been blown apart.

Laura told me how she was unhappily married to a marine there and that they had one son. She told me seductively how she used to be so naïve but had now become much more of her own woman. She had a boyfriend there, a Portuguese worker at the base, whom she talked to often on the phone in a sultry voice, planning their next rendezvous. After a couple weeks she asked me if I wanted to go out some weekend for a boat ride with her and her girlfriend. I declined her offer. Often, if no driving was needed, she let me go after lunch.

When I did drive the CO, Captain Allen, I brought the car around to the front of the building and there I stood next to the car at parade rest, waiting for the captain to come out. Once he was within ten yards of me, I stood at attention and saluted the man. He then gave me a quick salute. I would then drop my salute and open the back door for him. Sometimes he chose to sit in the front and we would chat a bit. At other times, we picked up a V.I.P at the airport and toured them around the base; then I usually brought them to the Officers' Club. He would instruct me when to pick them up or tell me that no more driving was needed; hence I would be done for the day. I did this job for a good month then it ended for I lost my driver's license due to a DUI (driving under the influence).

I had purchased myself a Honda Aero 50cc motor scooter for personal transportation on the base and one Saturday night I was stopped by the shore patrol which is like the navy's version of the police. I was driving back to the barracks after visiting the Leeward side of the base and a shore patrol car came swiftly around a corner, hogging the centerline, and crowding the middle of the road. I swerved to avoid them and they, in turn, turned around and caught up with me to pull me over. I passed all their sobriety tests, even walked on my hands to show them that I had all my balanced faculties, yet they still took me in to give me a breathalyzer test which I failed at .07% blood alcohol content. As a civilian this wouldn't be illegal, but the military's limit for drunk driving was .05%. I was furious for it was one Saturday night that I wasn't plastered and this happens! I automatically lost my driver's license for one year, rendering me unable to operate any heavy equipment as well.

Although it had been quite constant, my drinking now became more of a problem. I counted how many beers I had one weekend. I drank fifty beers over a twenty-four hour period, starting in the morning, Saturday, and not stopping until early Sunday morning. I was depressed, unhappy with being in the military, stuck on this rock; consequently, I was sent to an Alcohol Rehab Center in Orlando, Florida.

I left Gitmo one month short for my orders were for one year. I was airlifted out on a Medivac plane that carried various types of sick patients. There was a guy a few rows down who was in a straight jacket and he attempted to open the escape hatch while the plane was in flight! He was quickly overpowered by security and securely tied down in his seat where he babbled his craziness. I was admitted to the hospital at the navy base in Orlando where all of us drunks from various places in the navy, marines, and coast guard were sent to be cured.

Once again I lived in an open room with cots lined up side by side. We had to line up each morning and take a drug called Antabuse. It made one violently ill if alcohol was somehow snuck into the hospital and ingested. At first we only went outside to jog around a track and to exercise. This program was civilian run, headed by a woman who was an ex-drunk. It wasn't a militant atmosphere. Each part of the day was filled up with group therapy, psychodramas, movies and lectures, all about the disease of alcoholism. After the first week, we started going out into the town of Orlando to AA meetings.

The rehab was altogether an enlightening experience, despite the fact that I was kicked out of it. The idea that I was sick with a disease that most all the others there had as well, changed my perspective about drinking. It had initially been my way of having fun, but had turned more into a deviant crutch that I used to cope with life and its vicissitudes. The others there had similar experiences within their families, proving to me the commonality of this disease, that whole families were affected by it, whether its members drank alcohol or not. My father was an alcoholic and I certainly didn't want to wind up like him, a closet drunk. When we were kids, he used to regularly get up from his chair in the TV room, go into dining room, where his liquor cabinet was, and return back with a few wine stains on his shirt from chug-a-lugging his cheap port wine. My brother Chris and I used to steal the sugary stuff as pre-teens, getting shitfaced on just one tall glass. I knew I was an alcoholic from the start, but always was in denial of doing something about it, for I felt that I would suffer too much without it.

In group therapy I never broke down and cried like the others had, so my counselor thought I wasn't making progress in reforming; therefore, one day I was summoned into a room where the supervisor and my counselor were seated at one end of a long table. Once seated, I was asked if I knew why I was in there. I saw in my peripheral vision a door open behind me. A man yelled into my ear at close range, "Who the fuck do you think you are?" It was one of those ultra military Philippino guys who worked there more or less as security for the civilian counselors. He startled me terribly.

"Nothing more than the total sum of all of my parts." I calmly informed them all.

"You're terminated!" the supervisor said from way across the table. "You know that?" I didn't say anything. My counselor added a few demeaning remarks aimed at me, inferring that once released, I would run to the nearest bar to go get drunk. I refuted her statement, saying that I had changed over the last few weeks and that I truly wanted to stay sober. Regardless, I was discharged from the hospital after five weeks of the eight week program. I then reported to the Administrative Department of the hospital where there I found out what was to happen to me next.

Shuttled over to another part of the base, I gave my papers to the chief there, a good humored, bald, middle-aged man. He read my papers to me out loud. "Let's see…Terminated: Behavior Modification, Treatment Failure." He shuffled the papers neatly on his desk. "How was ARC?" he said to me, lifting his eyebrows and smiling, causing me to laugh.

"It was a drag." I said to him. "Now what happens to me?"

"Now we hang you!" he said straight faced. "Just kidding, I believe that you get discharged." Those words sounded so good to me. "You'll stay here until I find out. Okay?" For the next week I worked in the part of the hospital where terminally ill patients were kept; also there were navy personnel with mental illness, ones who somehow made it into the military but were now getting weeded out. I soon learned what was next for me for I wasn't getting discharged. I had new orders to go into a battalion.

I took a flight on TWA to Jerez, Spain where I was picked up at the airport and driven to the navy base at Rota, Spain to join up with the battalion that I now belonged to, NMCB 74. I reported to where the battalion was and was brought to my new barracks, a Quonset hut that a dozen or so of us shared. It had been over a year that I had been in the service and I had never had any privacy. I definitely wouldn't find any here for my locker only partially blocked my neighbor's view. I was in an emotionally fragile state, on the verge of a nervous breakdown. The absence of booze or any other drug was a new experience for me and I felt that at any moment I could break down and cry like a baby.

I took a good look at myself and my condition. I wasn't going hungry like I had earlier in New Orleans. I was in Southern Spain, it was February and warm outside, and most miraculously, I no longer wanted to drink alcohol any more!

The next morning I awoke early with everyone else and we headed out to morning muster, the usual role call that happened each morning. Being the EO that I was, I knew that I was supposed to be with Alpha Company, so I filed into the ranks with them. Still dark out, the CC called off his list of names and each guy says, "HERE." when his name is called. My name wasn't called! I should have reported to my CC and said that I was new there, but I didn't. I was uncounted and I saw a window of freedom for myself.

Once dismissed from muster, some go to their jobs; others might work later so they are free to go back to bed or whatever. I went back to the barracks, got into my civilian clothes and left the base to explore the town of Rota. At the end of the day, I went back to the base, had dinner at the Mess Hall, and then crashed in my bunk.

Next morning I got into my greens, went out for morning muster, and the same thing happened: my name wasn't on their list. It was great! I felt sort of invisible in the dark twilight of the dawn and I took full advantage of it. I went off the base again and went to a beach to get a good dose of some much needed solitude, meditating in the stillness of some sand dunes. I ran into some semi-girls who knew I was military person, since I spoke no Spanish and because of my high and tight haircut. They offered me some hashish to buy and gestured to have some fun by kissing into the air at me, but I wasn't interested and they let me be. I was on new path that was new to me for the other one I knew was a road to ruin.

The 15th of the month came up, payday for us in the military, and when I went to Alpha Co. to pick up my check they caught onto me. The chief EO really chewed me out. I told him how I wanted out of the Navy and that I should have been discharged, since I hadn't completed ARC. He loudly told me that I couldn't just quit for I had signed a five year contract. Like most EO chiefs, he was a marginally intelligent Fred Flintstone type. He had a booming voice and he angrily gave me my new job. I was to be a waiter at the Officers' Ward Room, a special name given to the officers' mess hall.

I worked with the cooks and one other Seabee, a steelworker named Finkes, a guy who, like me, was equally disenchanted with the Navy. It was not such a bad job for I only worked fifteen days a month. It was two days on, three days off, three days on, two days off, staggered between the two of us. There were only a dozen or so officers and their "Ward Room" was just a spiffed up Quonset hut. They ate much better food than we did as enlisted men, and the cook and I were able to eat what was left over. At dinner, the cook and I brought out the food and they served themselves buffet style. I later walked around with a tray of food to serve them seconds if they desired; in between I stood at parade rest near the kitchen door.

Officers in the military are usually people from wealthier families, most all having college degrees. Any officer outranks every enlisted man and all enlisted must address officers as "Sir". Often new recruits will call a chief or senior chief "Sir" and they usually say back, "Don't call me sir. I work for a living!" It's noticeably silly when you see a middle aged chief calling a neophyte officer "Sir". This is the way it is in the military, a hierarchal system with the chain of command.

Many of the officers I served were nice people, thanking me each time I served them; yet there were other ones who thought me to be some sort of servant or something, an underling who they enjoyed their dominance over. They were the spoiled rich kids that I was all too familiar with, having grown up going to private schools. They enjoyed their power within the system and most likely they joined the military so that they could have dominion over others. I saw these types of people as less developed, almost impoverished souls. Their need to dominate, as I understood it, was because they lacked direction and control of themselves internally, rendering themselves unable to empathetically relate to their fellow man. This military system wasn't all that much different than the capitalist system, for both fostered a type of artificial pride that was more divisive to the society than it was cohesive. In the military rank is what matters, determining your place in the hierarchy. To many in our civilian, capitalist system, it is status, wealth and possessions that are sought after in so called "success." Our own country's promotion of acquisitiveness and greed, where the ones who accumulate the most are the ones at the top, is wrong and it is one of the reasons why the world is being ruined. It is why terrorists from nonsecular countries drove planes into the World Trade Center. It is a way of thinking and behaving that we are going to have to outgrow universally as a species.

I had a lot of free time so I immersed myself in my art, doing pen and pencil drawings while sitting on my bunk. I opened my locker door to create a partition for added privacy but wasn't very effective for most guys walking by would peer around the door to see what I was up to. It wasn't unlike growing up in a big family where closed doors stirred up a curiosity as to what was going on in there. Opened doors didn't. My art became a type of occupational therapy that eased my mental discomfort. I was going through a slow transformation, a painful surrender, a dissolving, an implosion, all due to the vacuum that occurred inside of me from the absence of filling myself with intoxicants. In this loneliness, I had become a compulsive drawer. The others there thought I was mad. I was!

I rarely went out into the town with others for there was always a lot of drinking, nor did I like the attitude the locals had toward us military personnel, which was understandable. Somehow, we, the USA, had acquired this desirable location, the only forested area in this grassy region of Southern Spain. I also noticed there to be anti American sentiment there, such as in a billboard that showed Ronald Reagan next to large rocket missiles. I often walked off on my own to a nearby beach where I sat alone and thought. Thought which isolates as itself, a prisoner of its own making.

Sometimes I did go out and once I went with some guys to a casino about ten miles away. Most all of us lost our money, discouraging any further visits for most; but I went back other times and played blackjack. I loved to gamble. I'm naturally competitive and taking chances made things exciting to me, regardless of the consequences. I also enjoyed looking at the sleek, dark-haired women who were dealers there.

There was one gambler there, a man forty or so, who played roulette and often won big. His face was scarred horribly like he had suffered severe burns at some point. He had a beautiful girlfriend at his side who organized all the chips that he won. As the wheel turned, his head did too, in little circles like he was focusing on numbers; then, as the last seconds allowing wagering approached, he plopped down his sizeable bets, often hitting the mark and winning! Piles of chips came back to him, which his concubine stacked neatly while he sat there with a dead stare, waiting for the next spin. He seemed to me to be some denizen of some hellish dimension, where some deal was made to allow him to succeed at this chosen sin.

I, on the other hand, had lost hundreds of dollars on my visits, luckily to regain my losses when I won big on my last visit before we left to return to the states.

Battalions deploy half the year then stay at homeport for the other half. Our homeport for NMCB 74 was Gulfport, so we went back there again. It was June and incredibly hot and humid there. At homeport one doesn't have to do that much: "muster and make it" was a phrase use to describe its easiness.

I wanted out of the Navy but was unable to just quit so I decided to get kicked out. I intentionally didn't show up for morning muster and I was "wrote up" or put on report, hence I had to go to Captain's mast, an impersonal meeting with the CO of the battalion. It is like going to court only he's the judge and the jury. Dressed in your dress whites, you walk up to him seated at his desk, salute, take your cover (hat) off, then he reads your offense. Mine was UA (unauthorized absence). I told him that I wanted to get out of the Navy and he serenely pointed out that with my contract, I was government property and was unable to just quit. He dished out my punishment: 30 days and $300.

I was then ushered to restriction, a type of base detention prison. We were known as "restrictoids" there and we lived in a Quonset hut way in a far corner of the base where we could see alligators and water moccasins in a stream that ran right by the hut. It was oppressively hot in there, no AC or fans. We were woken up at 5am for inspections each morning, all of us standing beside our well made bunks that lined the walls of the open room. Some of us got stoned in the early morning, smoking joints in the shower since the heavy steam of that room would cancel out any smoke and smell of the pot. It was in this restriction that I met the most normal people, other free thinkers who found themselves stuck in the NAVY (Never Again Volunteer Yourself). After inspection, we all fell in outside in front of the hut to march together to chow; after which, we reported to our companies and they had us for the day.

During homeport there wasn't all that much to do for work. The construction work done on the base was contracted by civilian union workers. One week we did build a little town out in the woods. It was all portable with houses, electricity, even plumbing and running water with water tower. After five days of assembling this town we disassembled it. It was practice in case something like this was needed in a war. We also had to attend a few training schools and classes. One was for general math and we all were given a 100 question multiple choice test of simple math, geometry and algebra to see if it was necessary to take the class. I got a 100% on mine and they thought that maybe I had cheated, so I had to retake it while being watched, getting a 98% the second time. The stupid Seabee who had been watching me said to his chief, "You see, he cheated!"

"No man, he knows his math." the chief told him. I didn't have to attend the classes so I fell through the cracks, being an unattended restrictoid that week. Being in restriction, I wasn't allowed to leave the base, but one day I did. I rented a car at a car rental just outside the gates of the base and I went to New Orleans to Carrondelet St. to visit some friends there, telling them that I was a prisoner who had escaped for the day. I drove back in time to make chow where we restrictoids regrouped to march back to the restriction hut.

I had to go back to captain's mast twice more, for I knew the policy: three strikes and you're out. I did the same thing, I was intentionally UA for morning muster and I received the same punishment each time. It was miserably hot and humid in the Mississippian summer. I developed jungle rot or athlete's foot from constantly wearing boots. I also contracted crabs that clung to the roots of my pubic hairs. The base doctor gave me a special shampoo to kill them and a walking chit as well, allowing me to wear sneakers while the anti-fungus ointment healed my feet. He also gave me sympathetic support toward my plight, remarking that he too was looking forward to becoming a civilian again.

I caught flack once from a chief who saw me walking around in my casual tennis shoes. "Why aren't you in your boots?" he said to me as we passed each other outside.

"Because I have athlete's foot," I said and showed him the chit I carried in my pocket.

"Well so do I!" he said without looking closely to read the chit.

"Do you want to see my feet?" I offered for they were a gruesome sight.

"No!" he said angrily, "and get a haircut!"

At last my military career was over. I was discharged with an OTH (other than honorable) discharge which leaves me unable to ever be employed by the US government again. They didn't even allow me to keep all the uniforms that I had bought with my own money. I really didn't care. I was free again. How wonderful it felt, walking out the gates of the base carrying all my belongings in a seabag strapped over my back. But now what? It was mid fall and I had no particular place to go to, no home that I could return to. I decided to catch a bus back to New Orleans to get an apartment there for it was close and I had already lived there, plus it was warmer there for the winter compared to up north where it was far more expensive and freezing cold.

3
A migratory Life

Back in New Orleans, I first stayed with my friend Pete at his place on Carrondelet St., sleeping on a hammock that he strung across his living room. He had a little apartment perched up in an old carriage house that viewed a courtyard below where large banana trees grew, their huge green leaves looming just outside his window that had little crystal prisms hanging down on strings, casting rainbows onto the interior walls of the room when the morning sun shone through. He was a humbled, meek sort of fellow, an Irish Catholic like me. He was from Cleveland and had gone to Notre Dame. He moved to New Orleans after college and had been here ever since. He was helpful and generous to me, always had marijuana, and became sort of a spiritual guide to me for he had a library that possessed many religious books that I was ripe for reading, such as ones by Thomas Merton, Alan Watts, Thich Nhat Han, and Krishnamurhti. He had a ping pong table in the garage below and we played often while I was there.

I found a cheap apartment on Phillip St near the St. Thomas Housing Project, just outside an area known as the Irish Channel. It was an upper unit of a shotgun, an affordable but rather dilapidated place at just $160 a month. I fixed it up, painting the floors black and white stripes and the walls pastel abstract designs. I had a narrow balcony which had a bullet lodged in its railing, a telltale sign of the street violence nearby.

I spent the next months making paintings, almost all abstract ones that just sort of occurred automatically with little concentration on my part. I had a few thousand dollars from saving my earnings in the military, so I didn't look for a job. I avoided my old haunts because I no longer drank. I regularly walked over to Pete's where I met some others around the complex where he lived, people from other states who now lived in New Orleans.

Once, in late spring, when I was heading on a bus back to my place, I met a guy that I had known in my old neighborhood a few years prior. He was Harvey and he had dated the same girl I did, Manya. He had been rather kind to me at times back then like when, knowing that I was alone, he brought me leftover turkey and stuffing that his mother had made at Thanksgiving. When I got off the bus I figured that it was okay if I showed him my new place. He got a kick out of how I now lived right next to the projects. He came in and we talked a while. I regrettably showed him the two almost matured pot plants that I was growing on my balcony. He said that everyone had wondered what had happened to me. I told him about how it was that I didn't drink anymore and that I didn't want him to bring others over. I said that I would come uptown to visit them at some point. He left my apartment and I thought nothing of it.

About two weeks later, very late at night, I heard someone outside trying to climb up my balcony. Leaving the lights off, I grabbed a hammer and approached the intruder in the dark. I confronted him just as he was about to crawl over the railing. It was Harvey and he reeked of alcohol. "Trying to steal my plants Harvey?" I said to him as he froze, hanging onto the outside of the railing, crouching his head down the way dogs do when they're about to be hit. I knew that this guy could be trouble, that he might even have a pistol or something; but I didn't want to push him off the balcony for he could have suffered a fatal injury if he landed on the wrought iron fence below. I decided to try to coax him out through my apartment to let him out the front door. He feigned to be staggering and once inside, he put his hand on my shoulder like he was off balance and couldn't stand. In an instant he came quickly with a knife in his other hand in an overhand stab. I moved my head back trying to dodge him but he still caught me with his knife in a shallow penetration around my cheekbone. I instantly swung the hammer I held hidden behind my back, hitting him with a minimal blow with the side of the hammer for I didn't want to hurt him, only to subdue him.

"Motherfucker!" he said to me as he wobbled from my blow. He held out his knife feebly, pointing it in my direction like he was going to try to stab me again.

"I'll hit you again!" I threatened. He said nothing else for he was faint and blood was dripping down the side of his face and onto the floor. I gripped his arm and twisted it behind his back, causing the knife to drop onto the floor. On the verge of passing out, he was easily guided out the front door and into the stairwell. I locked the door and then called the police, telling them that I had been attacked in my apartment. I heard Harvey moving around in the stairwell and I told him the police were coming.

"You're the one going to jail motherfucker!" he said in a slurred voice. The pot plants! I scampered about hiding little seedlings I had in cupboards and I uprooted the two bigger ones on the balcony, throwing them into them into the dark where they landed in a hedge of my neighbor's below. I noticed that Harvey had now made his way down the stairwell and he was sitting on the bottom step, waiting for the cops with his shirt tied up like a turban around his head for a bandage. Over a half hour passed and still the cops hadn't showed up. He waited no longer, got up and staggered down the alley to the street and yelled up to me, "You gots me tonight!" he cried out, inferring retribution. Minutes later the police showed up. I told them what had happened as they gazed around the colored walls of my pad, that this guy had climbed up my balcony to break in and that I knew who he was. They were very skeptical and one guy freely searched my place while the other one talked to me.

"Have you ever been to jail?" one cop asked me.

"Yes," I said, "but the charges were dropped." He called in to have my name checked out and then told me that I had been arrested for carrying a pistol. "No. It was a fishing knife," I corrected him. I looked into the other room and saw the other cop opening and closing my cupboards.

"Why isn't there any blood inside here where you said you hit him?" the interrogating cop asked me as he pointed to the larger red puddle on the floor outside my door.

"There is. You see here!" I went down and pointed to a few reddish drops on the black and white floor.

"Maybe that's yours!" he said noticing the stab wound on the side of my face.

"What's this?" said the other cop as he came out with a little marijuana seedling he had found in a cupboard.

"A tomato?" I winced.

"No, we know what this is and you're a dope dealer and this is some kind of dope deal gone wrong. We see this stuff all the time."

"Look, I'm not a dope dealer. I just grow a couple little plants to smoke myself and I don't go around causing trouble or anything."

"Well it's illegal and we can arrest you for this. When did this thing happen anyways?" the cop asked me.

"About an hour ago. I called right after it happened."

"That explains the false call at 814 St. Philip," one cop told the other. In a strange coincidence the computer calling system for 911 had sent some cops to another street in the city called Saint Philip. Had they promptly came to my place on Philip St., Harvey would have been waiting to tell them any kind of story he wanted. Luckily, they didn't arrest me, and they even gave me a ride down to Charity Hospital where I got my wound stitched up.

After this event, I didn't want to stay in the city for I didn't feel safe any longer and summer was approaching so I headed back to New England on the train.

This time I knew better not to ask my dad if I could come. I just showed up. Fortunately, Chris and Eliza were there and since I hadn't seen either of them all for a couple years, I wasn't told to go away by my dad. I informed only my siblings about what had happened back in New Orleans and they were shocked but glad I was okay. I wouldn't have told my dad about something like this because it would only exacerbate further alienation. My family was rather unfamiliar with what sort of life I had led in the last few years, but they were all glad to hear that I no longer drank. I was back in the house that I had grown up in but it definitely wasn't my home anymore. I felt more like an intruder.

Dad and Wendy had been married for six years now. We all had known her formerly as Mrs. King, a woman from our same town, Manchester, whose children had attended the same private school that we had gone to, Brookwood School. She used to drive a white Mercedes convertible sports car and I remember as a youngster once passing her in the car with my mom and my mom said mockingly, "There goes Wendy!" as she whizzed by our station wagon. Wendy was divorced and once my mother died, she snagged my dad quickly, marrying him within a year. It was great for my dad because he needed a partner to cook and to help take care of little Eliza. Her kids adapted rather well to their mom's new scene. They had other step families on their dad's side. They even had ex-steps! Our father treated her kids even better than us for there wasn't any baggage from the past. We were all long out of the house, having lived off at boarding schools and colleges, returning only on holidays to increasingly odd scenarios.

All went smoothly with my surprise visit and I told my dad I was going to Maine, meaning North Haven. He said that it was alright, but only for the month of June. I made my way there on a bus from Boston. It was a four hour ride to a coastal town, Rockland, where one takes a ferry to the island twelve miles out. North Haven's a beautiful island with splendid scenery for painting. I had recently missed a couple summers there, but I had perennially visited the island with the whole family each August.

As kids in the 60's, our mother loaded all of us into the station wagon that was packed to the brim. Duffle bags, boxes and groceries were neatly positioned, allowing small areas for all six of us to sit. Back then, we even brought the two cats and our dog too! The cats didn't like the trip much. One retired under the driver's seat for the duration, making a most uncat-like moan. The other cat panted like a dog. Daddy usually followed up later in his Mustang.

Our house on the island was right on the water, literally. A wharf house remodeled since its earliest days of catering to the big schooners, the cargo ships of the era. The house was a long rectangular, cedar shingled, two storied triplex that balanced on wooden pilings and granite blocks. At high tide the ocean comes entirely under the house, making it feel like you're on a boat. My grandparents, my dad's parents, purchased this place back in the late 1930's for they had learned about the island through friends. We called them Ma and Pa and they lived at one end of the house with their live-in Irish cook, Sheila. The walls of their interior were water stained pine paneling with half round covering each spacing grove of the vertical boards. Nice old Chinese carved reliefs made by an eccentric white man a century earlier, were mounted as inlays on these walls, giving the rooms an Asian touch. Dad and Wendy now resided in this unit, the east house, for our grandparents had long since past away. The opposite end of the house, a four bedroom unit, was where we stayed in as children. The in between area, a three bedroom unit, was known as the middle house. All these units were under the same roof, a unique antique house that easily accommodated the likes of a large family like ours.

It was a bustling place in the summer, the center of all the action for we shared the wharf's space with a yacht club that occurred there for the months of July and August. The vicinity was known as "the Casino" which was accessed from the street by walking down some granite steps that led through a cubby hole that cut through our house onto the boardwalk pier that extended fifty yards or so out to a house that was the yacht club itself. It was a great place for kids. We all had done sailing class there and we could play in the numerous rowboats and outboards that were tied up right there in front of our house. We also did many family picnics to the various nearby islands that dotted Penobscot Bay.

I was now there in June before the onslaught of summer people, so it was very quiet and private. The house had smells that summoned back memories of my mother and our family. I had enough art supplies and I started making paintings that I knew I could sell later that summer for I had already sold dozens of oil paintings in the years prior at an annual art show for the island library, selling my first there at age twelve. I enjoyed the solitude and freshness of this place but pressing me was the fact that I had to find a place to live and a job for I was out of money.

My cousin Charlie was on the island and I caught up with him. He had heard about me being in the navy and everything and he wondered why, thinking me to be some sort of patriot or something. I filled him in with a summary of my life and how it was my reckless ways and my financial scene that had landed me in the navy and that I was in a similar situation at this point-no money and nowhere to go. He told me that he was currently looking for a house to buy in Roxbury, to fix up and to re-sell at a profit; adding that if I wanted to, I could stay there and work on it until it was done.

I wondered how it was that Charlie was able to buy a house for he was just a couple years older than I and he wasn't even employed. He divulged how he had inherited $100,000 from Ma, our mutual grandmother, a few years earlier. "Didn't you get any?" he asked with surprise. I hadn't and I explained to him that my four older siblings had indeed inherited a bunch of stocks that they all cashed in totaling about $28,000. Charlie had one brother which explained why he got considerably more.

I had often protested to my father about not getting this money. Initially, I inquired about it before I went into the navy and he, at that point, said that I would get mine when I turned twenty-five. Now I was over twenty-five and his current remark was that I had inherited nothing from Ma. Without any clout regarding his policy, I brought my disturbance to my siblings hoping that they could influence Dad's decisions, but their declarations about what they had been given were all different now. George had told me that he did get $28,000. Regrettably, he had blown it all on cocaine, adding that he had even told our father about this. It was no wonder that Dad might think that I would do the same if I was given the money. The others gave me diminishing accounts of how much they got: Dinah saying that she got $15,000.; Susan said $12,000., adding that all of it went to her shrink, as if that was some consolation on my part; and lastly Carrie claimed that she got a mere $8,000. My griping was to no avail and it only led to further agitation all around. Consequently, I remained, in the years to come, like most others who are not benefactors of rich families, bouncing here and there in a subordinate position to whomever I worked for.

I learned carpentry over the next few years and I stayed there in Boston area after my stint in Roxbury with Charlie. My next place was a little basement apartment in the South End near Boston City Hospital. While living there, I found a carpentry job in the Back Bay working with Irish immigrants who taught me finish work. I also managed to get some paintings done in my dim lit apartment which I was able to exhibit in a restaurant on Newbury St.

After about a year there, I moved over to Brookline where a friend from high school also had a wondrous ability to buy houses, fix them up and re-sell them at a good profit. We called him "Nutty" in high school due to his volatile temper. I rented a room in a rooming house that he owned and he employed as well as a renovator. He was a bit of a hacker as a carpenter but a hard worker. We were quite different for he was a bit of a "rightwinger," a guy who liked Reagan and the Republican agenda. I tried to avoid political discussions with him to keep from getting into arguments. Working for him was good because it was flexible and there were breaks between jobs, allowing me more time to make paintings.

I started painting more in the realistic mode using photos that I had taken. I also did portraits. Within the city area I saw many attractive women and I started approaching some with photos of some of my paintings, asking them if I could paint them. Many who I approached were wary, but some took me up on my offer. I did about a dozen portraits, often giving them away to the women if they wanted them. Two of them slept with me!

It was at this time that I became involved with a Buddhist group. One day, while in downtown Boston, I approached this attractive woman who was on her lunch break. I did my portrait thing, showing her photos of some paintings. She told me that she was in this Buddhist group and that I should come to check it out. Her name was Daria, a dark skinned woman about ten years older than I. Out of curiosity, and attraction to her, I went to this Buddhist place and met her again there. I liked Buddhism and had read up quite a bit on Eastern religions ever since I had quit drinking. I liked the atmosphere there and the fact that it was a multiracial group. I joined and was a part of the Franklin Park group, but mainly I was interested in this thing because I liked her. We went to different members houses and chanted together.

Buddhism is a different sort of religion from the Christianity that I knew about. This one was Mahayana, one main branch of the religion. I learned that there is nothing supernatural about this religion, though it may seem so from its variety of sects. It's more a psychology that analyzes the world as being in a constant state of flux where everything is interrelated. Our modern physics has proven that all physical objects are made up of tiny particles that are constantly moving, at the atomic level and beyond, like a swarm of bees moving at close to the speed of light. Our limited perceptions of the world don't allow us to see these things. This was understood long ago and this understanding of constant change overflows into the individual, who is constantly changing as well. Creating a better understanding of the self is helpful in liberating a person from suffering, which is caused by erroneous views. "Pain is inevitable, but suffering is optional." said the historical Buddha. If properly comprehended, one can escape suffering which is a byproduct of the self, of which, there is no corresponding reality other than itself!

I learned about a Buddhist format of experiencing things in a relative way: the ten worlds. World one is hell or the worst thing we can feel. The next worlds move upwards, defined accordingly up to ten which is enlightenment, the best world. The insight is that within each world, one can experience any of the other worlds. This rang true for me, for I had become keener at watching myself, my impulsively generated feelings, and there were times when I did experience bliss within horrible conditions; or on the contrary, a deepened sadness in an extremely wonderful situation. It is difficult to understand this relative nature of our subjective, internal experiences until we have noticed and experienced them for ourselves.

The culture of the West, of which I was born into, tends to dictate to us early in our lives that the world is a multiplicity of separate things, extending that erroneous view that the individual is separate from everything else when, in actuality, they truly are not. Possessions are sought after, obtained and held as our own. Properties become "mine" as do mates, children, and social groups. The things added to each individual are attempts to console their aloneness, consequently creating a larger barrier to the understanding that nothing is "theirs." Things are added right up until the end when they run into the horrific conclusion that they're going to lose all of it! In all its good intentions, this secular lifestyle collides with the spiritual one. Things like solitude, silence, stillness, and emptiness become sad and unfortunate things to them. To me, the spiritual, non-secular way of life is more advanced one, where one does not add things but rather weeds out and subtracts until the self created boundaries are gone. It is only then that we can experience that we are no longer isolated separate beings, but one with the ground of all existence!

I stuck with the Buddhist group for a few months, but the practice of uttering the long Chinese liturgy and chanting for extended periods of time, wasn't for me. I like all religions and I study the aspects of each that I learn about, seeing this common denominator in all of them: everything is one thing.

Summer came along and I painted a few more seascapes and scenes at North Haven, which I was able to sell later in August. My stays there on the island were never very long. Two weeks was the maximum that my dad allowed me there, and that shrunk until I wasn't allowed there at all! This stemmed from the ongoing conflicts between us and it headed off when I confronted him about his drinking. I wanted to help him. I knew that if he were able to stop, to understand his own drug addiction, he would turn against it, the same way he that he found cigarette smoking to be utterly vulgar, now that he had been hypnotized to quit after forty years of chain smoking.

We, from alcoholic families, have a tendency to be drinkers. My mom didn't even drink; consequently, my dad nicknamed her "Carrie" after the prohibitionist, Carry Nation. The results were that she adopted this name, dropping her former: Helen. Mom had expressed to me that both her parents were drinkers and she felt that if she drank alcohol that she would be an alcoholic as well. This was one galvanizing facts that I re-learned in rehab and I wasn't bashful about letting my father know this.

At North Haven, Dad had his regular routine. He walked out of his house onto the dock and into the middle house, where he had his workshop area and his stash of booze, always hidden under some rags in his paint closet. There he took his doses of bourbon or whatever. One evening at twilight, while I was there at the house, I was inside the middle house, down in the adjacent room to his workshop, when he came lumbering in. He didn't notice me there. I stood there silently and watched him down some booze from his bottle. After a mild gag, he spotted me there standing just ten feet away. "Now cut that out!" he said, startled and in utter embarrassment.

"You know, the only reason I don't drink anymore is because I know I would wind up like you." He sneered at me behind his thick glasses. His lips curled inward making his mouth very small.

"Cut it out!" he cried again, this time in more of a growl. He then exited with heavy thumping steps, swerving a little as he made it to the door, leaving me standing in that room that all of the sudden seemed to become very dark. The next morning he told me to leave. I asked him why and he said, "Because you're a pain in the ass!"

"I want to help you! You really should stop drinking." I told him calmly, trying not to turn this into an argument. He laughed mockingly at me and didn't say anything.

"You don't tell us what to do!" said his wife Wendy who was lingering in the doorway of their house, listening to us. It was around 11am and she was still in her nightgown. I left on the next boat and grabbed the bus back to Boston.

Once in my room at the rooming house, I called some of my siblings on the phone, relaying why I wouldn't be seeing them in Maine for they were to visit there shortly. The older sisters exclaimed that I mustn't do things like that and that I can't change people. On the contrary, I felt that I could change people; moreover, that I could influence people to want to change themselves for I had personally been changed by others. It was through AA meetings and other people getting on my case that made me want to change some of my destructive my habits. I felt it my duty to get on my father's case because no one else ever did. None of my siblings ever encroached on Dad. It was taboo to them.

That fall I went to Belize, Central America. I had always wanted to go to Central America and I had enough earnings saved to sponsor myself a painting trip there. I had heard about the place from some guys in New Orleans who went there to dive on the coral reefs off the coast. I liked the idea that there was an English speaking Caribbean population there, and I still had a penchant for black women.

I started out where the plane landed, in Belize City, which turned out to be rather dangerous, but I got away unscathed. At the airport, it was like Kingston, lots of young men trying to earn a buck with the few tourists who came into their country. I found a cab driver and asked him if he could take me somewhere where I could find a room to rent. We went to someone's house he knew but no rooms were available, so he dropped me off at a cheap hotel right in the downtown area. I got a room there and then walked around to check things out. It was rather difficult walking about for I was hassled by panhandlers and others who wanted to tour me around. I gave in to one guy, letting him tour me for he kept following me around anyway. He had nasty slice marks on his face, scars from a machete fight or something like that. He gathered that I had come to paint, so he took me to a gallery where a middle aged Englishman sculpted driftwood into abstract designs.

We then went to a bar that overlooked the river that flowed through the town, out into the harbor. He was puzzled as to why I didn't drink as I bought him a beer and a soda for myself. As we sat there longer, he questioned me more as to why I was in his country. I could sense more of his hostile intent toward me. Some other guys gathered around me, the foreigner. A very tall fellow put his hand out to me, offering to shake my hand and he said, "Remember me!"

"No." I thought he was inferring that we had met before.

"Remember me!" he said again with a sinister smile. My guide got into his face and forced him off me, for in truth, he wanted me as his sole scam victim. I felt unsafe there and I got up to try to leave but my guide now wanted me to give him $20 for his services. I gave him $10 and he wanted more. Then another heavy set man, who was plastered, walked over to where I stood. He carried a bottle in one hand and his other fist was clenched. Slurring angry things at me, he leaned his sweaty forehead against mine like he was about to punch me. Again the scar faced friend of mine had some words with him and we both left the joint. I gave him $10 more and it still didn't satisfy him, but I just kept walking away without talking and he left me alone. I went back to my rented room.

That night I went to a bar in town where lots of girls were. Quite a few young British soldiers were in there and the girls seemed to pair up with the most of them. I found a nice girl in there and brought her back to my little room. It was hot and humid and we showered together in the lukewarm water that was the same temperature as the air.

The next day I caught a ride on a little skiff out to Cay Caulker, an island about fifteen miles away. It was rather shallow all the way out there, with coral reefs and turquoise colored waters where white sand was under the ocean's wind-swept choppy surface. I found a peaceful beachside, thatch-roofed cabin out there on the little island. I made some paintings each day, walking with my canvas and paints to various locations on the island. At night I looked for action but it was out of season and not many people were there. After a couple weeks, I went back to the mainland and explored more.

When it was time to go, I caught the plane back to Boston, first stopping in New York to visit my sisters. Two of them had jobs at NBC. Dinah worked at Saturday Night Live and Carrie worked for David Letterman. I went to shootings of both. Susan also lived in the city and her first book, Monkeys, is a big success. It's a book using different accounts from our childhood. Mum sometimes called us little ones "monkeys." She kept the same first letter of our names for our ficti-tious characters. In one story, my character, Sherman, is in a car accident while drunk and he makes a big scene back at the house. She writes her account of what happened even though she, in reality, was not there. When I saw her at a get together at Carrie's, Sue goes, "I'm starting to see what Sam's going to look like as a man." My sisters were sort of passive aggressive types to me for liked to dish out mildly diminishing remarks to boost their own egos. Susan had been through years of depression and years of expensive therapy, covered mostly by our wealthy aunts. It was nice to see them but I had become very different than they were, having led a very different life.

Once back in Brookline, I went back to work with Nutty on his latest house. Just one other guy worked with us and one day Nutty threw a fit at him. It was one of those violent temper tantrums of yelling and screaming that left the other guy stunned. It shocked me too, so I walked off the job. While I was walking away he said to me, "What's wrong, I never did anything to you!"

Back at the rooming house I learned from the others that I was being charged a bit more for my room than they were. I called the Brookline Housing Authority and found out I was paying $100 more than the rent controlled amount he was supposed to be charging. I told this to Nutty and he went into a bit of tirade again saying, "I really don't like you and if you don't leave I'm going to call the police!" his voice becoming like that of a child with a lisp. Gladly, I would get out of there, away from this nut! I had been there too long and it was time to move on. It was December and I wasn't fond of the long cold winters up there, so I headed back south to Louisiana. I called Pete and found out there was an apart-ment at the Carrondelet St. compound where he lived.

I took the 36 hour train ride back to New Orleans and was welcomed by the balmy weather. I got a nice apartment, a three roomed place with high ceilings and lots of windows, a good place for me to paint. The rent was just $300 a month, easily half of what I would be paying back in Boston. One drawback of this place was that it was on the ground floor, vulnerable to thieves; but, I had nothing to be stolen.

I painted often, making up plants with a surreal twist. One was of a potted, thorny stemmed, green leafed plant that had a green eye wrapped into its middle. Snail antlers protruded from the plant at the top. I entitled it: "Protection from Sickness". My neighbor, a Guatemalan man, bought it and commissioned a portrait as well. Another painting was of a rhubarb-like stemmed plant that grew out of a little island of sand, surrounded by tropical waters. At the end of each stem was a leaf split down the middle, resembling lily pad leaves. Once finished, I counted how many leaves it had: twenty-nine, the same as my age. I called it Aquarian, as for I am Aquarius.

I adopted a black cat that was around, or he sort of adopted me as his owner since I fed him the most. He was already known as Baby Night, a thin black cat, incredibly agile, a bit of a showboat. I decided to teach him a trick, a trick that I had seen an old man on North Haven do years ago with his cat, Blacky. Each evening when I fed him, I put my arms in a loop so that the cat had to go through them to get his food. I did this low on the ground first, then as time went by, I did it higher and he would jump through my arms. He was smart and learned rather quickly, happily jumping higher and higher. A few months later he would come in hungry and just start jumping at my hips.

Months later, my cat was missing and I worried for no one had seen him. Then one day, I heard some kids in a parking lot next door. A young girl was telling her little brother to stop throwing rocks at it. It was Baby Night. He had been injured for he dragged himself along the ground, crawling with his front paws, his legs splayed out. I thought perhaps he had been hit by a car. I had to wait until morning to take him to the Vet. The next morning a friend with a car took us to the Vet and we dropped the cat off. Later the Vet called me up, telling me the cat had been x-rayed and that a 22 caliber bullet was lodged in its spine.

There were a lot of guns in this city and one could often hear them being fired late at night in little battles in the ghettos beyond. On New Year's Eve everybody liked unloading their firearm into the sky, making it a danger to walk outside because of the raining bullets.

Crime was rampant in New Orleans. The city often ran neck and neck with Detroit for having the country's highest murder rate. I was held up once, ten years earlier when I worked for that plumber. A guy was preying on victims who came out of a bank on a Friday afternoon. He stuck his pistol in my face and told me to hand over my wallet I obliged but asked him if I could keep my driver's license, knowing the hassle it would be if I had to get a new one. He consequently grabbed all the cash, my meager week's pay of $130, and then handed me back my wallet and told me to run. I turned around and walked at first until he said, "I said run!" I did.

One other day, I was walking up Carrondelet St. and a smartly dressed brother in a hat, vest and sunglasses, came around a corner and almost bumped into me. He then jumped into a white sedan that was parked there waiting for him. They gave me a funny look before they took off down the street, so I glanced at their license plate and got the number. I continued to where I was going, an abandoned lot on St. Charles where deep in the back amongst the overgrown vegetation, I had some pot plants growing. Once there, I picked some leaves and tops, shoved them into my pockets, then headed back to my place, this time walking down St. Charles, the wider avenue lined with live oaks. A streetcar went down the avenue's middle, the neutral ground that divided the car traffic on both sides. I noticed a few police cars and a group of bystanders outside a bank, my bank where I had my savings account. I noticed one of the tellers there and I asked her what had happened. She told me that they had just been robbed.

"Did this happen about fifteen minutes ago?" I asked her. She nodded that it had. I directed my speech to a cop who stood there next to her. "I think I saw the guy who did this!" I told him, but it didn't really mean anything to him for lots of people saw him. I added more. "No, I mean I saw the guy get into their car over at Harmony and Carrondelet and I remember their plate number." At this news he was enthused and he got the plain clothed detective who came over to me with a slight smile on his face.

"You saw the plates? What were they?" the detective said, jotting down what I told him. He called in this information then started asking me some questions. "Where were you going?" He asked, looking at me from head to toe. I got a little nervous when his eyes stopped at my pockets for they were filled with the illegal leaves.

"I was going to the store," I told him.

"What did you get? You're not carrying anything."

"Thinking quickly, I said, "I just dropped off some film at K&B to get developed." My hands pushed at my pockets to make sure the pot leaves weren't sticking out. His radio was called on and they informed him that the plate numbers I had given them matched for a car in the city.

"Well, maybe we got a lucky break this time!" he said to the other cops. "Where do you live son?" he asked me.

"I live at 2821 Carrondelet."

"I'm going to send over a detective to pick you up in about a half an hour to see if you can ID this car alright?" He patted me on the shoulder.

"Okay," I said and walked back to my apartment. I regretted having involved myself. What did I care if these guys robbed a bank! Regardless, half an hour later, an unmarked police car pulled up in front of my house and honked the horn. I came out and got into his car. The guy was a fat middle-aged fellow with thick glasses. He offered me some coffee as we drove off. I noticed the stained thermos next to his ash tray. Thanking him, I declined his offer. He said we were going over to the Ninth Ward to see if we could find this car I had seen.

"So what was the make?"

"What do you mean?" I asked, not understanding how to tell cars apart.

"Yeah, I guess that's something you learn…how 'bout you point out a car that it looks like if you see one, alright."

We continued along Washington Avenue, going through the Harmony Housing Project where many people were out and about. Little kids played dangerously close to the traffic on the street. "It was like that one!" I said pointing to a car parked on the curbside.

"That's a GM," he informed me. We finally made it across town to the Ninth Ward, came to the street address that matched my declared plate number, and saw there in the driveway a Toyota with my plate number. It obviously wasn't the same car that I had seen. The detective drove me home and thanked me for my help.

Back in Massachusetts, my dad had retired from his job at the bank, and he had sold our house. They were moving to Santa Barbara where Wendy's mom lived. I heard about there being a huge yard sale at our house, where all items there were up for grabs. My siblings and steps were allowed to cart off anything they could and the rest was sold. Of course I wanted items, yet was unable to make the trip there to get anything; and where would I stay even if I could have made it there? I was barely selling enough paintings to cover my rent. I stayed in New Orleans all summer, enduring the oppressive heat with a little fan that blew across my body as I slept naked and sheetless on my bed. I did a few Maine seascapes and sent them to my father at North Haven, asking him if he would try to sell them for me. He did, sending me back checks from various buyers, but no included note from him.

My father was a banker with a conservative Republican background. It was known to us in our family that in the 1960 Presidential Election, our mom had made him a bet that her candidate, Kennedy, would defeat his, Nixon. The result was our black and white dining room floor. On topics such as nuclear power, his bottom line was, "You like your hot water shower, don't you?" I let him in on alternative, friendlier ways of getting hot water. He would chuckle at me in a mocking way as though I was ignorant of all that took place in the world. Our conflicts mounted as years went by. I understood that much of his demeanor and his personal choices were that of a person molded by his upbringing. He was from a wealthy Bostonian family that extended a dozen generations back in America. He was sent off to boarding school in sixth grade and probably liked it better than his dull homestead. However, he was a bit of a nonconformist within his own class for he married an Irish Catholic woman, something quite radical for the time. We are all extensions of our parents and my nonconformist ways were partially inherited from him, just taken a little further down the road. Additionally, I carried his self-destructive ways too, and that amplified as well!

Since I didn't make much money selling paintings, and I barely covered my rent each month, I fell casualty to my ever present gambling habit. If I was down to just $100 I took $80 of it to the track with the hopes that I could multiply it into more; but most oftenly, it was lost. After losing, food was scarce again and I became depressed for it was entirely my fault, done by my own free will. There was that element of hope each time I gambled that beckoned me back.

The majority of people you see at a race track, or other gambling places, are the regulars, the compulsive gamblers who keep playing over and over until their money is all gone. There's an excitement, a kind of high as well that comes when chances are taken. This, no doubt, is part of the physical addiction that we get, causing this "jones," or this urge, to gamble again and again. We don't gamble to lose, but we don't mind losing. It's part of this self-destructive tendency that we have.

I looked up GA (Gamblers Anonymous) in the phonebook and called them for I wanted to get better. There was a message on a phone machine instructing me to leave just my first name and a number that I could be reached at. I did this and later a man called me back, introducing himself as Fred. His voice was like that of a gambler, low and scruffy, like he had been a card shark or something. He thanked me for calling and asked if I had ever been to a meeting before. I hadn't. He proceeded to tell me where the meetings were, on Airline Highway in Metairie. It was quite far away, over an hour, and I had to catch a bus there down at Canal St.

Strange Poverty of the Rich

The meeting was in a conference room at a hotel near the airport and I arrived there just as the meeting was getting under way. It was similar to AA, for it was the same twelve step program. We all said the serenity prayer then an elderly, gray-haired, sage of a man walked up to the podium. He welcomed all of us then said the shocking line, "There are two ways out of this: you can come here to the meetings or you can die!" I thought this to be a little steep, but I noticed that some others in there nodded their heads in agreement. He went on to give some facts about this "invisible disease" as he dubbed it.

All the things he said was so true. I never showed the anguish I had felt from losing all the money I had earned, and I never could tell others about this for they wouldn't understand why I kept doing it. Often in the past, when I became destitute, I had asked my dad or my sisters for money, but they too knew that I was probably scheming for gambling money. Knowledge of my gambling also jeopardized any chance that I might get the family money that the others had. This sort of thing made it that I had to keep it all to myself; apparently, this was most common amongst us compulsive gamblers, hence defining it as this invisible disease. I saw the truth of how gambling pushed people into further isolation and despair, to suicide for some.

After the long talk, a few more things were added about future meetings. When it was over, a couple of people approached me, the youngest person in there. When the meeting began I had raised my hand when the man asked the group how many had come to their first meeting. They told me that I was lucky to be there and to keep coming back. I liked the meeting but I didn't come back. I did stop gambling for a while, concentrated on painting, and got a lucky break with a new gallery in the French Quarter.

The K&B drugstore chain has a large art collection at its headquarters at Lee Circle and one time I brought in a painting of a Magazine St. Po'Boy shop to try to sell. The director bought it for their collection! Months later, when destitute again, I brought in another. This time the director referred me to someone she knew who was opening up a gallery in the Quarter. I called her friend on the phone then I brought down a couple pieces to show him. He instantly took me in and fronted me some money, writing me a check for $1,000. He wasn't exactly my kind of guy, about sixty, wealthy from inheritance, from Meridian, Ms. When I met him, we sat at a café across the street from his new gallery. He made mild passes at me, testing the waters of my sexuality. His wife was there; but she was inside the gallery while we talked. They had an Andy Warhol portrait of her in there.

I was inspired to make more paintings, now that I had a marketing outlet. I did oil paintings of the cemeteries, the live oaks in the parks, and scenes in the Garden District. I brought them in to him where I determined my prices. There was a 50% cut with each sale and he sold a few of my paintings, but he cut my prices without telling me. I didn't like this, for I felt I could sell my paintings at the same prices that he sold them for. I stopped bringing in my paintings. He argued that we had to start low in order to build up a reputation for the collectors. Maybe so, but I wasn't interested in playing this game for some future financial gain that shared my profits with some elitist fool! I tried to retrieve all my paintings but he kept some as collateral to my debt.

Once summer rolled around again, I wanted to go back north to Maine. I wrote my dad, asking him if I could go to the house at North Haven. He wrote back saying that I could go and stay there at his house for two weeks in June, since I hadn't been there the year before. It was quite far away for me to go for just two weeks. I planned on going there for three or four months! I gave up my apartment, leaving some of my stuff in Pete's garage to reclaim when I came back in the fall.

I took a bus all the way up to Maine at the end of May. Having depleted my savings, I made it through the month of June with very little money. I bought enough art supplies to make more and more paintings so that I could sell them later that summer. Once my money was entirely gone, I resorted to eating the foods that were stockpiled in my stepmother's kitchen.

Dad and Wendy arrived for their summer stay in early July and he wasn't happy to see me that I was there. "You've deliberately disobeyed me!" he told me, since my stay there obviously lasted more than two weeks.

"Well, I haven't been here for a couple years and it gets incredibly hot down there in New Orleans. Would you rather me to be there making paintings of Maine there, to send back here for you to sell for me like last year?"

"Yes!" he said. Wendy looked down at the floor and sighed.

"I have to be here for Chris's and Carrie's weddings later this summer. I can't afford to fly back and forth. I don't have any money!"

"This is true George," Wendy said to him.

The next day Dad told me that I could stay. Elated, I offered myself to do any work, for the house needed a lot of maintenance. I stayed in the opposite house, made many paintings and sold more that summer than I ever had so far. He and I got along fine. We played golf together at the island's nine hole golf course, and I even had dinner with them at times. I stayed entirely out of his way, never mentioning anything about his addiction to alcohol.

The two family weddings occurred later that summer. First, Chris was married in an Episcopal church on North Haven in late August. His bride, Fannie, was another summer person whom Chris had known his whole life, but had gotten to know better in his late twenties. He had the alcoholic infliction as well, having totaled two cars and one boat before he was sixteen! He also had a knack of having rich girlfriends who supported him. The breakup of his last partner left him clamoring for another one. Fanny fit the part, for she was from a rich family and was a corporate lawyer as well. The reception was at her grandmother's on the island, followed by a dinner and dance down on the wharf at our house. The newlyweds left at dusk in the Boston Whaler for their honeymoon out on an island, Resolution, while the rest of us continued the party on the docks until Dad, with a small towel partially wrapped around his waist, commanded from his balcony, at about midnight, for everyone to go home.

The next weekend was Carrie's wedding and that was at the Hamptons on Long Island. They too were married in an Episcopal church, the groom was a divorcee and she had difficulties in locating a Catholic church to accommodate their wedding. The dinner and reception was at a country club, the Maidstone, a castle-like stone building propped up right on the sandy coastline. Before dinner got underway, everyone was ordered to vacate the premises for there had been a bomb scare. The police took it very seriously, perhaps because Caroline Kennedy was there. A helicopter hovered overhead and hoards of policemen showed up in a bus. We all were instructed by a cop on a bullhorn to get a certain distance away from the building, pushing the crowd out onto the golf course fairways where the party continued. Golf carts came out loaded with champagne and the band members played their acoustic instruments amongst the scattering of well dressed friends and family members who stood on the dark green grass that was contrasted by a beautiful pink sunset. It turned out to be quite nice, much to the chagrin of the culprit responsible for the bomb scare; who, incidentally, was never caught, but thought by all to be the groom's ex-wife!

I stayed in Maine until the end of September; then headed back to old New Orleans where I found another apartment in the same Carrondelet St. area, but in a different building, an old brick one where a huge magnolia tree grew in the front yard. It protruded like a giant umbrella over the building's front portion, shading the balconies that were held up by ornate wrought iron works. My apartment was in the rear of the building, sheltered from the street, overlooking a lovely garden and courtyard that was inlayed with a brick patio. There were often little parties out in the patio where we often shared meals. Most all of others living there were drinkers, and I tended to get alienated once they got drunk, since I didn't drink. I did still smoke pot though, but was perfectly content without it.

Ever since I had quit drinking, I had to be wary of hanging around people who I recognized as being alcoholics. The personal reformation or revolution that I had gone through wasn't something that ever would be over with or completed. It was ongoing. I would always be a reforming alcoholic. I was very cautious and receptive to alcoholism in others. I noticed that other alcoholics, at times, tended to belittle me and negate my choice of not drinking. It is our human nature to find solace with others in our own folly. As a man at AA meeting wisely pointed out, "It is like a basket of crabs: the ones that try to crawl out get pulled back in by the others."

I kept painting away and had to market my own work. I randomly spotted big houses in the Garden District and I made paintings of them, later ringing the doorbell of the house with my painting in hand to try to sell to them. If this didn't work, I carried my completed paintings around to the antique shops on Magazine St. with the attempt to sell there. This didn't work, but in one shop a man, who was a customer, told me he would buy my painting and he asked me if he could see more of my work. I invited him, Gene, over to my apartment to view more paintings and he liked them. Telling me that he didn't have much cash available, he referred me to a friend of his named Herb, who was a dealer with antiques and old paintings. Herb had a shop on St. Charles and Gene often did business with him. Herb liked my paintings too. It worked out well. Whenever I was out of money, I now had a place a place to swap a painting for cash; though it wasn't ever very much. Herb was a shrewd businessman and a bit of a shyster, for he resold my paintings at a good profit. I am not a stickler and only want what I immediately need for money, so I was a pushover to him. The less he paid me, the greater his profit.

I continued my gambling at the track with the extra money from my sales. Having learned my lesson, I stocked up on food and art supplies before I blew my money again. I would go over to the Fairgrounds, wasting my time and money on the horses, getting a little bit of social interaction by seeing all the people on the busses and at the track. Once the money was gone, I had no choice but to stay at home and paint. It was at this time that I started playing the keyboard.

I loved the music in the city and I always wished that I were a musician, for it is such a powerful art form. I had seen the various groups playing at the Jazz Fest and I particularly admired the Gospel Tent where local groups played. The simple down to earth spirituals hit me head on and blew me away, like a type of spiritual wildfire that caught my soul, burning up the pain and remorse that I can acquired in my life. It was like grieving when my mother died. Within the despair, there is recognition of the love that is there, love that is divine and universal. This is something that this soulful music could reveal to me, for I am fortunate enough to have the ears that can hear it. It also inspired me more to be the artist that I am.

I am compelled to live my life as an artist, not for financial gain or fame, but more for religious reasons. The wonder of beauty and the mystery of life command me to do something to share this, to spread it to anyone with eyes that can see. Beauty exists because of its symbiotic relationship with love. We can, metaphorically, liken beauty to waves and love to the wind: the more it blows, the bigger and stronger they get. There are deep congruencies between art and religion. When I was a youngster, my mother predicted to me that I was going to be a priest. I had seen those boring gray haired priests at church and I thought how awful that would be, not understanding then that the life of a solitary artist was indeed like that of a monk's.

Once summer arrived and the hot humid air pushed down on me, I migrated back to Maine, despite having received a letter from my dad that told me not to go to there. I knew his house was off limits, so I rented for the month of June from a friend who had a house on North Haven. I painted without any distractions for very few people are on the island before summer sets in. I had a good thing going there on that island, being able to sell my work to make a living as an artist and I wasn't about to let my father's policy towards me destroy that.

One day, in late June, a miraculous thing happened to me. In the morning, I went over to the nine hole golf course on the island to play a few holes. I ventured into an area where my grandfather used to have a little vegetable garden. He was instrumental in the early days with this golf course, and had acquired a plot to garden up there near the course. It was quiet and pleasant in there, sheltered by tall spruce trees. I picked some asparagus that still grew in there and I ate them raw. As I was leaving the garden, I paused and looked back to examine the wooded spruce perimeter for I felt as though I was being watched. I saw no one there and I continued on back to my rental to plan my day's painting excursion.

I organized my paints and stuff and went over to the Casino where the boat was. I walked by my brother Chris, who was over at our house for a couple weeks while his wife worked in New York City. I told him I was heading out in the boat to go paint.

"Dad told me not to let you use the whaler." he said, obviously having reported to Dad that I was on the island.

"How's Daddy gonna know?" I asked him while I continued walking down the dock.

"I'll tell him!" he said in a wimpy, childish voice.

"You do that, pal!" I responded angrily and continued down the wharf to get in the boat that was tied up at the dock. He watched me while sitting up on the balcony.

My destination was Burnt Island, an island owned by our family. It had been purchased by our grandparents, purportedly for just hundreds of dollars back after the Great Depression, during a time when owning a spruce covered island seemed ludicrous. On my way there, while skimming across the waves on the Boston Whaler, I pondered how it was that I got to come to this place, solely because I was born into this rich family. I thought more of my grandfather, Pa, whom had died when I was just twelve. I wondered what his relationship was like with my father. I arrived at Burnt and tied up to the float. I knew where I was going to paint, at a little bog just behind the rocky beach, where wild irises bloomed at this time of year.

I walked down a little path that was blanketed with spruce needles and cones when suddenly, a little red squirrel sounded off its flickering reel. It was right there about a yard in front of me on a branch. I stopped and we looked at each other in the eyes. I felt as though I was being greeted by Pa's spirit that was within this squirrel. I pressed on a few more steps, and upon my first steps onto the beach I found a magnificent arrowhead, perfectly formed, about four inches long! It was a wonderfully spiritual experience for me, a confirmation, a gift from my grandfather. I did my painting while standing in the bog with the purple flowers all around me; then I returned back to the Casino in the whaler.

On the dock at the Casino I ran into my dad's sister, Aunt Ellen. She admired my new painting, noticing where I had done it from. I pulled out the Indian arrowhead and showed it to her, telling her how I had just found it.

"Sounds like your grandfather left it there for you!" she said.

"Yes, I think so." I had heard stories about how he used to get arrowheads, either finding them himself or buying them somewhere, to place on the beach in front of his guests, so that they could have the thrill of finding one for themselves. I showed Chris too and I wondered why he hadn't seen it on the beach for he had been there a couple of times already. It was mid afternoon and he had a beer in his hand, already a little drunk. I headed back to my rental down the street.

Soon Dad and Wendy arrived. I went over to their house to say hello to them. They both are quite unhappy that I am there on the island. "I told you to stay away from North Haven and you've gone right ahead and disobeyed me!" he said angrily. "And don't use my boat!"

"I'm not staying in your house. I'm free to come and go to this island just as you are." They both sat there quietly not knowing what to say. "I hear from the sisters that you've stopped drinking!" I said a little louder than I normally talk. The sisters were regularly invited out to Santa Barbara for Christmas, the guys weren't. It had been reported to me that Dad had been ordered, by his doctor, to quit drinking for he now had become a diabetic from the boozing.

Wendy answered for him, "Yes, your father stopped drinking last fall." He sat there next to her with a phony smile on his face.

"Does he feel better being sober?" I asked her while I looked at him with that disturbing smile etched on his face. She didn't reply. I waited a moment then said, "Well that's terrific! See you all around!" I walked out, knowing that it was a complete farce for he looked sicker and older than ever. His nose had become sort of purple and his eyes were glazy behind his glasses. Later that week I went over and checked his normal drinking spot in the Middle House. Sure enough, there was a newly drained bottle of whiskey in there.

The rents on North Haven are very steep during the prime summer months of July and August and I needed to find a place to stay. Out on Burnt Island there's this ramshackle shack, an old kit house assembled back in the 1930s when my dad was a boy. I fixed it up enough so that I could live in it, fixing holes in the roof, replacing floorboards and adding a couple of windows that I had found discarded at the town dump. I also found there, a queen-sized mattress which I brought out to the shack and put on a platform I made out of driftwood boards which I found along the island's beaches. There had been a farmhouse at this site one hundred years prior and a well was still there which I was able to use for my fresh water. Apple trees still grew just off in the woods and an old rhubarb plant made its annual showing out front amidst the raspberry bushes. It was a pristine, country setting that became a sanctuary for me.

One day in mid July I was painting on the beach at Burnt and my cousins, my dad's brother's family, came out for a picnic. They came over to inspect my painting and I mentioned how nice a place this was to paint, adding that I hoped we could build a solid house out there someday.

"Haven't you heard? It has been given to the town!" my cousin Bebe told me.

"You're kidding!"

"Hasn't your father told you?" she asked with surprise. He hadn't mentioned anything about this to any of us. I was furious to hear this. I decided to go over and pay my dad a visit.

Being out on this island and without a boat, I was able to get to and from North Haven by walking across the mud flats at low tide. The tides are rather steep in this part of the world, about ten feet. They change from high to low twice per day. Burnt Island is a true island only at high tide, for at low tide there is an isthmus of mud and rocks connected to North Haven. I placed big flat rocks along the muddy spots so that I could traverse the two hundred yard passage without getting my feet dirty. I kept my bicycle stashed in the bushes on the North Haven side; so I got on it and I rode back into town to our house where I found my dad in his workshop in the middle house.

"I heard from the cousins that you all have given away Burnt Island. Why didn't you tell us about this?" I asked.

"Because it's none of your business," he curtly answered without looking at me, carrying on with his business.

"That's a valuable asset for our family. Why couldn't we keep it?"

"If you want an island go buy your own!" he said, now looking at me, his nose pointing upward in snobby way so that he could look down at me. This really ticked me off, for I had previously heard from my cousin Charlie that the island had been left to us grandchildren so that no inheritance tax would be levied. My dad and his brother were the executers of her will and I felt something was definitely fishy.

"It wasn't yours to give away." I said and he ignored me, like I wasn't there. I changed the subject. "That's a total lie that you've stopped drinking. I know what's going on in there," I said, pointing on in towards his paint closet area to refresh his memory.

"Go back to wherever you came from!" he said to me in a stern monotone and a blank stare. I stood there right in front of him and silently looked into his eyes. "Go away!" He stomped out of the room and onto the dock, back over to his house, to the sanctuary of his wife, who was somewhere in there. Beautiful Maine, and she seemed always to be indoors!

My brother George came to North Haven and stayed at our house for a few weeks with Dad's permission. I rarely saw him and was glad to see him but I noticed that he had changed a bit. He had been living for quite a while in New York City and was heavily involved in psychotherapy there. He preached to me that the only way to salvation was through this psychotherapy, and that I must do it too. I informed him how I had been through a transformation as well, six years prior, and that I had stopped drinking. I also informed him that the rumor that Dad had stopped drinking was not true. I mentioned as well that Burnt Island had been given to the town.

George is a writer and as we talked he jotted things down, for I informed him of some of my past experiences as well as the more current conflicts that I had with Dad. I was curious about his novel for he did have a contract with a publisher. At first, he was reluctant to tell me about it, then after a few days he leaked a little and I learned that he was writing about me! My name in his novel is Simon. It's a twisted version of who I am, turning me into a more sinister person who kills the father. I wanted to see some of his book, <u>The Blue Bowl</u>, for I could sense that it was more or less a vengeful type of thing on his part, done because he was envious of me and what I could do.

I sold thirty eight paintings that summer, the most I had sold so far, despite the difficulties I had encountered being banished by my father. Most of the paintings I did that year were quite small for I didn't have access to a car or boat. I made a little box that held 8"/10" painting surfaces, so that I could carry it around unharmed in a knapsack as I rode my bike around to paint different scenes on the island. I rented gallery space for one week and sold most all of them. Dad came in the gallery the last day of my show, strolling with his hands behind his back, noticing that I had sold most all of my paintings.

"That must make you happy to have sold all of these," he said as he exited. Some people walked by him outside and commented to him that I had done some very good work. "Thank you!" he said to them with pride, as though what I could do was something of his. This bothered me. I noticed it to be a pattern in the other things that he thought to be his own.

I noticed that this possessive way of thinking was more commonplace amongst the rich, a byproduct of our social system that promotes ownership. We, in this system, learn young to be owners. As babies we cry when others use our toys, though our parents try to teach us to share. In wealthy families, the toys often pile up and we lose interest in them, but always want new ones. Christmas is the favorite time of year because more things become ours. Amongst the poor and less privileged, kids don't always have things the same way. A simple item like a basketball is more in the stewardship of one to be used by everybody. Sharing is a characteristic that isn't imposed by the parents, like in the rich families, it is natural and beneficial to the individual to co-exist with his peers or he'll be alienated by the group. Amongst the rich more boundaries are created, hence a more divided society that they live in.

I stayed in Cambridge that winter. My step-sister Lisa informed me that an apartment was available in the house she lived in near Harvard Square. I rented it, the smallest apartment I had ever lived in, the most expensive one too. The standard of living in the area was like a whole country removed from New

Orleans. I tried to keep painting but my place was so cramped that the fumes from the oil paints made it most unpleasant in there. Lisa suggested that I get some studio space, but that cost money and I was running out of the money I had made, so I had to look for a job. Lisa worked for the Cambridge Housing Authority and she told me of a job position as a janitor with one of her clients, CASCAP, housing for disabled people. It was just $8.00 per hour but I took it anyway, since I was in need of a job and money.

I started working right away at the St. Paul's Residence, a building right in the midst of Harvard Square that CASCAP leased from Harvard. My supervisor was a nun, Sister Virginia, and she explained to me the things that I had to do, mostly cleaning. Each day I cleaned the bathrooms, vacuumed the floors, emptied the trash, and cleaned up around the outside of the building. Virginia made it clear to the tenants that certain rules had to be followed, or they would be evicted. There was a waiting list of many others who wanted to live there. She instructed me to report any empties found, for drinking alcohol there was prohibited. Once my chores were completed, I helped her out wherever she needed help.

Sr. Virginia was about fifty years old and she had a few college degrees, one a masters in Gerontology. She told me that most of her career as a nun had been working with the elderly. She was Irish Catholic from Brooklyn, New York and she had a bit of a Brooklyn accent. She lived there in the building as the manager. The tenants were people with different disorders: some with chronic illnesses, some mentally impaired, and others with physical handicaps. I was surprised how intolerant Virginia became, at times, with some difficult people, so I had to mediate their arguments.

Some residents there were really difficult cases. One elderly woman, who had gone senile in her old, didn't like Virginia very much; but, she was fond of me. As I worked in the hallway she often called out my name, "Samuel, Samuel, Samuel." She rambled on to herself while she sat out in the common area and I couldn't help but listen to her. Sometimes there was insightful wisdom in the things that she said to herself, like "I just like to sit back and watch people make decisions." or "I knew it was coming...you can't undo what's already been done." I wondered what she had done to have gone off into the deep end like she had. She had five children. I saw three of them there visiting and they seemed perfectly normal.

Another fellow in the residence always said to me, "Time to make the donuts." whenever he saw me, referring to a TV commercial for Dunkin Donuts. He was about fifty years old and once I told him that I was an artist, he told me he was too. Inviting me into his room, he showed me his stuff-piles and piles of typing paper with scribbled pencil markings, minimalist modern art...I guess. This man told big fibs as well, like saying that he had worked for the FBI and that he had an artist's agent who sold his work. Virginia didn't like the paper piling up in his room, a fire hazard since he was a chain smoker as well. Strangely, the only place they could smoke was in their room.

We had daily lunches at the residence which I helped set up. We tried recruiting other elderly people in the neighborhood, but few ever came. It was an odd mix of people for many weren't mentally disabled, but they seemed to cope well with those that were, for everyone there shared the fact that they were dependent on others for help.

Well into the year we received a new tenant, Jim, a young guy who had fallen out of a window while very drunk at a party and had consequently become a paraplegic. He was heavily into AA and he convinced me to come to some of his group's meetings. Jim got terribly depressed at times. Virginia had divulged to me that he had attempted to commit suicide before, and that I should keep a close eye on him. He had been this way less than a year and understandably couldn't cope. At times he lost it in frustration at attempts to open a door or to do something that he no longer could do, ending in a wail of tears that spread to some of us who were watching him.

At Christmas that year I was alone. My sisters went out to Santa Barbara. I wasn't invited to go there, nor could I have afforded a plane ticket out there anyway. It snowed frequently and I had to go down to St. Paul's whenever it did, to shovel out around the building. Virginia also referred me to some of her nun friends to shovel out snow around their houses, earning me a little more money which I still tended to squander at weekend trips to the race track.

I had no girlfriends, but I enjoyed seeing the pretty college girls while I walked from my apartment down to St. Paul's. There was one woman I saw occasionally whom I had a distant crush on. She was a volunteer at the St. Vincent de Paul's lunch for homeless people that occurred at the church across the street from St. Paul's. Bringing over leftovers from our under attended lunches, I got to see her, Italian by her looks, brown eyes and dark hair cut to her shoulders. She was a bit older than I, fifty or so, but she was attractive to me, timelessly youthful. I knew the attraction was mutual because she changed her tempo when she saw me. Once, when she was giving me a bag, our hands touched and she stayed there and looked closely into my eyes and smiled. At Christmas, she came over to St. Paul's to give extra cake from her side and she kissed me softly on my cheek. I knew she was married and nothing ever happened between us.

At the end of May I quit my job, for I wanted to go back and paint and spend the summer again at North Haven. I stayed in our house, hoping that I might go unnoticed there for June; but since I had told Lisa that I was going to Maine, it leaked to Dad that I was there. In the middle of the month he called on the phone and angrily told me to get out of his house. I lied to him, saying that I was in the same rental down the street and that I had just come over to the house to get something. He ordered me to go back to my job, to ask them to re-hire me. I told him it wasn't a very good job and that I earned far more money selling my paintings there at North Haven.

"You can't just keep painting pictures for the rest of your life," he advised.

"Well, I'm going to try. It's what I want do!" I told him.

Our caretaker for the house on North Haven was familiar with this conflict between us. She understood that I needed to stay somewhere and she was even glad that someone used the house for it was almost always empty! I told her that I would be elsewhere for July and she let me stay in my family's house without informing anybody. Dad and Wendy arrived in July for their two month stay. I stayed out at the shack on Burnt again, did my gallery rental for a week, and sold a bunch more of my paintings. I avoided the Casino and my father, seeing him only in haphazard passings around town.

In August, I went to Paris, France. My youngest sister Eliza, just out of college, was living there for a year and she had arranged for me to house sit there for a mutual friend of ours, who had a flat in the Montmarte section of Paris. I shared the flat for a month with this girl's big black cat. I saw Eliza only briefly for she went off to Ireland with a boyfriend of hers whom I wasn't very fond of; so I was alone in this nice old city. I did some more painting, selling two there, and I practiced my French at stores and cafes that I went to. I liked Paris, clean and organized, old and refined. After August in Paris, I went back to Maine for September. I decided to try New Mexico for that winter.

I packed up my navy seabag with clothes and my art supplies, bought a ticket to Albuquerque, and then took a shuttle van from there two Taos. I had never been there before nor did I have any plans arranged; so, I first got a hotel room there in the small town of Taos. I did know a couple of people who lived there, but they weren't very close friends, just people I knew. I looked in the phonebook and called one of them. He was Harry, Nutty's brother. He had a little Inn going and was putting an addition onto his little house. I had done a little carpentry with him back in Brookline, so he knew I could help him out. He drove over to town and picked me up in his little MG. He was going through a divorce and he had split custody with his two sons, five and eight years old. I stayed with him, sleeping on the pull-out futon couch and helped out any way I could, babysitting or booking customers for the Inn right there which he constructed as well, an adobe style building that was sunken into the side of a hill, facing south to maximize the solar heating, amongst the high Mesa, a treeless flat land covered with sagebrush just at the foot of some mountains where skiing was popular in the winters. I liked the climate there, dry and warm. The clouds appeared so separate from one another in the dry air, making for beautiful sunsets.

In my first week there, I had a strange encounter downtown. Harry let me use a bike and I rode it into the town plaza six miles away from his house, had some breakfast, and just took a walk through the town. As I went to retrieve my bicycle, a cop called me over to his squad car parked there. He ordered me to put my hands on the hood of his car; then he frisked me and took me in to the police station. I asked what was going on, but he remained silent with a sullen look on his face. Once at the police station, I was led into a windowless concrete room where he emptied his pockets and locked his revolver in a metal drawer. He was a Chicano man about my age and he was definitely pissed off at me for some reason. He proceeded to tell me that I had been identified as having done some graffiti in town and that a woman in the plaza said that I had been stalking her.

"This is some sort of misidentification. I wouldn't do things like that," I said, noticing his angry expression and clenched fist. "This is kind of scary!"

"I've never seen you before. What are you doing here in Taos?" I told him that I had just recently arrived, informing him where I was staying and that I was helping to do some work there. "Why aren't you working there now?" he asked.

"Because Harry's busy doing something else this morning," I said, being very polite, calling him sir, using my learned military talk. After further questioning, he told me that he couldn't hold me for formal charges hadn't been filed. He quietly drove me back to my bicycle. Once there, I offered a handshake as a gesture of friendship. He refused it and left me.

Weeks went by and things started to get hectic at Harry's. Like his brother, he had a bit of a temper and his frustrations mounted with his ex-wife whom he still wanted. When it was Harry's turn to have the kids for the week, he was often diverted to other things he wanted to do, leaving me to baby sit for his boys. Fortunately, Harry went to Colorado one week while the kids were at their mom's, giving me some solitude and time to paint. I did five or six paintings there. I loved the vistas to paint, but the rents there were way too steep for me and I didn't have a car to get around, so I decided to go elsewhere.

I only had about $900 in earnings left, didn't have any particular place to go live, so I returned to my old haunt in New Orleans, knowing that I could get a cheap rental there. I used a portion of my money for a plane ticket; then almost all the rest of it for the first and last month required to move into a new apartment. I had practically nothing. With no bed or mattress, I slept on my clothes. I sold all my New Mexico paintings to that dealer, Herb, who must have thought me to be a drug addict or something for he said, "I know you're hurting, Sam, so I'll buy them." Of course I wasn't a drug addict, but I was still an addict of sorts for what little money I did have, I kept gambling with. The city now had a gambling casino, a riverboat that was docked up at the Riverwalk downtown. I took my money there and played Blackjack, hoping to multiply my earnings, winning at times, but losing again soon thereafter.

By the end of January, I was out of money again and driving myself crazy from gambling. I was still sleeping on the floor in my empty apartment. Any one in their right mind would have at least bought a mattress or sleeping bag with their money; but I gambled and I lost it again. I didn't tell any of my friends there about the strange thing I was putting myself through, this invisible disease. I examined the postures of bums passed out down at Camp St. to see what the best way was to sleep on hard surfaces. It is lying on our sides. My rent was soon due and I didn't have it.

I remembered that I had a tax return coming to me from my job the year prior at CASCAP, so I contacted them and gave them my new address so I could get my W2 form sent to me. Once it arrived, I took it to one of those places that expedite tax returns by fronting a loan toward it. I got around $800 and went right back to the casino with it.

For a couple days, I gambled in there nonstop, until it was all gone. It was very early in the morning and I walked out of that riverboat feeling terrible. It was a cold dreary morning and the air even smelled toxic. I felt around in my pockets, hoping that I had stashed a $20 away, but I hadn't. I only had $3 to my name and my rent was overdue. I remembered that man in the GA meeting warning how gambling can kill, causing suicides. I briefly entertained the thought of robbing a bank, or something like that, to get me over this hurdle. But that was too crazy! I felt trapped, like I had been snared in a trap, no where to go, all the results of my own actions. I should have just walked down to the employment office and gotten a temporary labor job, but I didn't. I was lost in a way, ashamed of what I had done, sleeping well, having pleasant dreams, only to wake up in the morning with a feeling of dread due to this episode of compulsive gambling.

I called my father in Santa Barbara and told him that I was back in New Orleans, but that I was moving back north to Portland, Me. I asked him if he could send me a little money. Surely by this time, my dad thought of me as a complete nuisance; but he agreed to send me a little something since my birthday was just a few days away. I waited until his letter arrived. I fasted for I had no food at all. I did a couple of abstract paintings with the few colors that I had left. His letter came. It contained a check for $100. He always wrote his checks with numbers in both spots, rather than writing "one hundred" in the middle line as is instructed. I changed the ones into fours by adding an L onto the 1's. When I deposited it into my account, the teller took a second look at it then processed it through. The next day I was allowed to withdrawal $100. Since it was an out of state check, it took a few days to clear. I immediately went to the supermarket and bought some food for I was starving; then, I took the rest of the money back to the casino where I lost it all in about ten minutes, losing every single hand that I played. I waited the next few days for the forged check to clear, closed my account, and bought a train ticket to New York.

When I got to New York, I called Susan's but she was out of town. I called Eliza, who was there, and I spent the night on her couch. When I started to tell her about my gambling problem she sort of giggled, so I left it at that and just said I was moving to Portland, Me. I don't know why there, just a place, a destination to tell people. I didn't know anyone there, nor did I really want to live there. I was just inadvertently going, running away from chaos.

The next day I took a bus to Boston with the last of my money and I called my step-sister Lisa at work, telling her that I was in town heading for Portland. She invited me to spend the night, living now in Brookline with her new boyfriend, Lanny.

That evening at their place I told them about my mishaps from gambling and that I was totally broke. Lisa suggested that I buy a bus ticket to Portland with my credit card. I informed that I didn't have credit cards or any money at all. Lisa knew that I could do carpentry and she mentioned this to Lanny, who owned some tenement type apartments in East Boston, one of which had been vacant for a couple years. It was proposed that I could live there and fix it up at the same time, using my labor toward paying the rent. Lanny was a co-owner with another man, Frank, so he had to check if this would be okay. Meanwhile, being entirely broke, I asked Lisa for a loan. She said she couldn't loan me any money, knowing now that I was this compulsive gambler.

I called Carrie who lived in a mansion in Glenn Cove, Long Island. I asked her for a loan, telling her that I was at Lisa's and that I was broke and homeless. "You got to get out of there!" she advised me. I told her again that I had no money at all and that was why I needed a loan. Since it was a few days past my birthday she said she wanted to give me a birthday present anyway, so she would send me a check for $100. I told Lisa this money was coming so she, in turn, fronted me $30. A few days past and Carrie's check never came in the mail. Lisa became suspicious of this check that I claimed was coming so I called Carrie back to see what was up. "Oh my god Sam! I'm so sorry. I have a little baby and I hung up the phone and just forgot all about it." I needed her to confirm this with Lisa to prove I wasn't lying for I needed some money immediately since I could move over to East Boston into this vacant place of Lanny's. He had checked with his partner Frank and it was alright with him. Lisa gave me $70 more and Carrie wrote the check out to her and off I went to the slums of East Boston.

I talked to Frank on the phone and he told me to meet him at the Maverick Station subway stop in East Boston. I told him what I looked like and he picked me up there in his Isuzu jeep as I stood waiting outside the subway stop in East Boston, a place where I had never yet been. Frank was an Italian American from Easty, who now lived in Revere. He was curious why I wanted to live there, where we were going, but he didn't probe too deeply for he had a new worker that he could utilize. I just told him that I was totally broke. He didn't seem very fond of Lanny, calling him a "fat cat." It was an odd partnership for Lanny was a rich Jewish fellow and Frank a gangster-like towny.

We arrived at the house on Meridean Street, one of a row of brick houses that ran the entire block. Their building was a three story, three unit one with the vacant unit, the one I was to live in, on the ground floor. The other two upper apartments were occupied by Hispanic people. Most all of East Boston had become populated by immigrants from Central America and Southeast Asia. He asked me if I spoke Spanish then he laughed. We went down to the basement where he kept some tools that I could use. Also there, was a mattress that that we brought up that I could use to sleep on. As he left me in this empty, ratty place, and said to me with a grin, "You're roughing it!"

The apartment was three rooms long with a full bathroom and heat which Frank turned on for me. There was a gas stove in the kitchen area but no refrigerator. He brought one in a few days later. The first night I heard rats running in the walls. Fearing that they might come into my warming apartment while I slept, I rolled up some newspaper into balls to create a little barrier that enclosed my mattress which lay on the smelly wall-to-wall carpet. I did this so that I would be awakened if they encroached on my territory.

I started a big clean up the next day. Frank came back and dropped off some sheetrock and joint compound for me to repair the walls with. I agreed that I owed him fifty hours of work towards each month's rent and after that I could be paid a scant $8 per hour for the additional work I did. He owned a few other buildings and I did some interior painting in them as well.

After a while, my apartment was alright. It had a nice front room with three bay windows, allowing light to come in, good light for painting. Despite the honking horns, passing cars, and the strung out street walking prostitutes out on the sidewalk, I adapted to the inner city environment. There was a sliver of a view between the houses across the street, so I could see the harbor and the Bunker Hill Monument far off over in Charlestown.

One day, a large filling in one of my molars fell out when I was flossing, exposing a nerve. I needed a dentist badly. I had another tooth that had suffered a similar fate about a year earlier and it had since turned into a little black nub that no longer hurt. I walked around to various dentist offices in the area and they all required that I had to pay upon services rendered for I had no insurance of any kind. I needed two root canals and caps on my teeth, but that was rather expensive and I didn't have the money to pay for them. Consequently, I got my teeth pulled at $70 each. I could afford that much. The pain was gone but now I had two vacant spots in teeth that made chewing some foods very difficult. This was something I had to get use to for it was a couple years, until I later earned enough money to get bridges.

Late in Spring, I agreed to help Frank clean a summer house that he owned and rented out up at Lake Winnipesauke in New Hampshire. First we had dinner at an Italian restaurant where he knew almost everybody there. He had a couple beers then we made the two hour drive up to New Hampshire.

While driving, we talked and he mentioned that he had gone to Vietnam while in the Army. He explained to me how they were all young, foolish guys who were simply transplanted into the jungles of Indochina, adding that a platoon of fifteen of them was easily defeated by just 3 or 4 Vietcong.

"It was their home!" he told me, "We would just tromp through the woods looking for the enemy with our pots and pans clanging. They would tire us out by keeping us awake at night with noises and things. We were led on these wild goose chases that lasted for days; then they would eventually ambush us at night." He proceeded to tell me of a time when he thought he was a goner. "The enemy had dams on the rivers and streams and they would flood the jungles to try to drown us. Once the water kept rising and it went up to our waists while we were walking. Everybody panicked!" He was noticeably stirred from re-examining such intense memories. "Some guys wanted to climb trees but that was dangerous because of poisonous snakes and we'd be sitting ducks if they came around in their canoes. We had to keep moving to higher ground. We all carried a lot of weight and I fell into a hole or something and went under water. It was dark and I went in over my head. Flailing my arms around, I was about to run out of air, then one of my buddies reached down and grabbed my arm to pull me up." His hand wiped his face and his tearing eyes which stared straight ahead at the road. We got to the house and I cleaned up some rooms. We moved in some firewood and got the place ready for his tenants then we drove back to Boston.

That Summer, I went back and forth to Maine a few times, keeping my apartment in East Boston. I still wasn't allowed in my family's house so I did weekly rentals or stayed out in the cabin at Burnt Island. I did enough paintings to rent the gallery space again and I had a private show which earned me $8,000. I wasn't there at North Haven for August, so I missed seeing any of my siblings, for that was usually the only time in the year that I saw them.

Our differences had mounted over time for we led such different lives. The times we were together didn't seem all that pleasant for we tended to argue; or at least this seemed the case from my experiences. My different past and my perspective of society, which seemed to collided with theirs, was enough ground for the tension that sparked between us. When I said things like, "I don't like rich people," they found this to be a problem, something that was wrong with me; moreover, that it was an insinuation that I didn't like them! Most all of my brothers and sisters friends were other rich people they had met in their private sectors at prep school and college and they all seemed to keep within the same type that they were familiar with. To some of them, the richer a person was, the greater their so called friendship was. I recognized that they didn't know this to be wrong! Private schools don't churn out all that many people like me who don't want to be rich and materialistic; more frequently, they produce individuals who want to perpetuate their own institutions to keep themselves separate and distant from those who are less fortunate. Other things that interfered with our amicable relationship was baggage from the past concerning our mother's death.

Our mother was killed in a bizarre car accident, colliding in her car head on into a train that ran nearby our house in Manchester. She was forty-eight years old when it happened on that sunny, January Monday morning. It was deemed that the lights weren't working at the railroad tracks crossing due to an icy storm over the weekend. In any case, the engineer stated in the newspaper that he saw her coming down the hill and that he had sounded the train's horn. It was a direct head to head collision and her little Ford Fiesta was demolished, causing her instant death. The priest who blessed her body said that she had a content smile on her face; unlike he had ever seen on a corpse.

I was at boarding school when it happened and when I got home I told the others that I didn't think it was an accident. They were upset that I had such thoughts. However, Carrie and Susan proceeded to show me a bunch of poems that Mum had written down, all about death and dying. Also, written on her calendar, covering the days of Saturday and Sunday, was a quote that said, "If I am not satisfied with the death I have received, I shall return." I told the two older sisters something that Mum had told me months earlier and that she had confided in me not to tell anyone else. When Dad was in the hospital, getting a large goiter removed from his neck, she smuggled him in a bottle of whiskey upon his request. She said that she hated the fact that he was a drunk, but that she didn't want him to suffer. Upon hearing this news, my sisters got angry at me, claiming that such a thing had never happened. It wasn't until they mentioned this to our despondent father that he amazingly confirmed its truth, causing them to wonder why Mum would have told only me something like that. I knew of other problems that Mum had faced over the years, being married to an alcoholic, but she put up with it.

There were other recent occurrences that led me to think that something was awry with Mum. The last time I saw her was when she came to watch me play at a hockey game a few days before her accident. I saw her in the stands while I was playing, but after the game she was gone. This had never happened before. At her death, I reflected how it was that I had insulted her earlier that fall when she came to a soccer game and I said to her, "What are you doing here?"

"I came to see you!" she said with a sour look on her face. I was at an age of wanting independence, but I know I rudely insulted her by doing this. Many things were under the surface and all her children, except for Eliza, were out of the house. Her job as homemaker and mother of seven was pretty much over and the future prospects of living alone with an alcoholic must have depressed her. I don't know what happened. It could have been, and probably was, a freak coincidence for her Catholic upbringing surely shunned any thoughts of suicide since our lives aren't our own in belonging, but that of God's. Anyhow, my ideas about what had happened were taboo in the mentioning and this further vilified me, making me a difficulty within my family.

Later that year, in the fall, I called that guy Nutty in Brookline and told him I wanted to come over to visit. I went over and met him at the rooming house which he had now converted to a profitable inn, since the rent control laws had abated with the new Republican legislators in Massachusetts. I brought a couple paintings to show him, telling him that I was selling lots of them in the summer in Maine. He apologized for his previous behavior with me and even bought both of my paintings. I was in need of money again and I wanted to work for him again. He changed his mind the next day about the paintings he bought, but I kept the money towards work I did for him. I continued working for him that winter and did more paintings back at my apartment in Easty.

In February that year I got a commission to go paint at St. Thomas. Nutty had told me that a mutual friend of ours, Barney, was looking for an artist to go and paint their family's place at St. Thomas. I had known Barney since I was a child. He was from Manchester and we played on the same intramural hockey teams. I called him on the phone and then went in to his office in downtown Boston to meet him. Like most of my peers from childhood, Barney was from a wealthy family. His father had recently died and Barney was now president of the family business, Corning Capital, an investment banking firm with over one billion dollars in assets. I hadn't seen Barney since I was eighteen, but he seemed very much the same in his looks, a boyish looking fellow with effeminate features. There was a large framed photo behind his desk of himself in his Holy Cross College hockey uniform. A "C" on his uniform designated him as the captain. He told me that the estate at St. Thomas had been his grandfather's and that now he and all his cousins had to sell it; that's why he wanted an artist to go paint the area, for personal mementos of the place. I brought in with me to his office a bunch of photos of paintings and one larger rolled up oil painting to show him. He liked them and hired me on the spot. I mentioned that I didn't have any money to buy myself a ticket there, so he gladly agreed to purchase my ticket for me, upon which I would pay back towards the sales of my work. So, at the end of the month that February, I was off to paint on a tropical island in the Caribbean.

I was picked up at the airport in St. Thomas by the caretaker of the Corning's estate. He was Bill, a guy about my age who lived on the estate with his wife and two kids. The Cornings owned the entire Western tip of the island, a beautiful area with steep hills and lush with little trees and vegetation; as opposed to the more arid and developed side of the island which I saw driving from the airport. Bill took me to where I was to stay, a poolside cabana right on the shoreline of a cove known as Botany Bay. Large waves crashed on a coral reef near the little thatch roofed house that sat right on the edge of their swimming pool. The big waves were loud as they smashed against the hard cement-like coral shore. It was wonderfully pleasant at first, but as time went by the nonstop wave action's noise became a nuisance. At night as I slept I would be awakened thinking the crashing waves were a howling storm. After a few days, I had to walk a ways away from the pool area just to get some silence and to clear my head!

I was free to go anywhere I wished on their land to go paint. There was no mansion there, just small houses about the compound area where my cabana was amongst the tall palm trees and well kept grounds, tended to by black workers. I did thirteen paintings of various sizes in my ten day stay that had ideal weather. It was a solitary and inspiring experience due to the beauty I encountered as well as the money I knew I would make.

Once back home I brought the paintings into his office and he bought ten of them, earning me $6,000. Immediately I made dentist appointments to get my teeth fixed, for I finally could afford to get the work done. The bridges filled the gaps in my molars and I, once again, could chew my food properly.

At the end of May, I gave up my apartment in Easty and did the Maine island life again, living much of the time at Burnt Island. On occasions I stayed elsewhere or snuck into the empty family house to take a hot shower. My solitary lifestyle allowed for a great deal of focus on my painting and I was always able to sell just about everything I did there. I did get to see my siblings as they came to the island. I was still on Dad's shit list and wasn't welcomed in his house, but I saw the others on picnics or at nights that I stayed in town. My older sisters still liked to propagate, with Wendy's help, that Daddy had stopped drinking. He hadn't. I noticed him to weary, his body bloated and his nose had turned a dark reddish purple.

That Autumn I had to find a new place to live. I ended up sharing a rented house in Cambridge with one of my friends, Pete, who was also a summer person at North Haven. I moved in with him in October and bought my first car, a Jetta diesel, with the money I had earned from sales. I did exceptionally well that summer so I decided to go to Hawaii for a while at the end of October. A couple named Ken and Shaunagh Robbins, who had a summer place on North Haven, had bought a couple of paintings, and though I didn't hardly know them, they invited me to come visit beautiful Hawaii, so that I could paint there. Well, I took them up on their offer, left my car in the driveway of my place, and flew to Honolulu just as it was getting cold in Boston.

I arrived in Honolulu around midnight and had arranged to stay at first with someone else because the Robbins were off island. They had given me the number of a woman, Maeve, who was a friend of theirs and an artist as well. I had called Maeve back in Cambridge and had talked to her a little. I phoned her again at the airport in Honolulu to tell her I was coming. When the cab brought me to the address she had given me, she was standing there with folded arms outside on the curbside in the dark. She was a pale woman with blondish hair and blue eyes, an Irish woman my age who had lived in Hawaii now for six years. We walked up a little stairway that led to her small studio apartment. We smoked a little pot she had then we went to bed. I slept on the couch that was right next to her queen-sized bed.

We got better acquainted the next day. She was from Dublin and from a family of seven just like I was. She showed me some of her artwork: Hawaiian themes in watercolors; designs looking a little like Matisse. She was having a hard time making a living there because the cost of living was so expensive. I showed her some photos of my paintings and explained that I planned on painting Hawaii for a couple months. She already knew this anyways for most of the stuff I brought with me was my art supplies. I didn't find her particularly attractive, but she was nice and she had a curvaceous figure. Out walking on the next evening, we kissed then slept together in her bed. The following morning she told me of a dream she had: A tiger was outside in the bushes, she pointed out the window, and it walked back and forth looking for a way to get in; then it jumped through the window and made love to her. We both laughed.

The Robbins returned and I moved into their guest house, an apartment over their garage apart from their house in the Kahala section of Honolulu. Ken was a trial lawyer who had his own practice and had rarely lost a case. Shaunagh worked there in his office too. Both of them were in their late fifties, overtly social and moderate drinkers, neither of which I was. But I got to know them each night when they came home from work. During the days, I went out and painted, using an old Toyota to drive around that they had for their guests.

I explored Oahu and Maeve often came along, the both of us making paintings. It was an extraordinarily beautiful place. The light in the sky manifest itself into beautiful rainbows and other visual spectacles. The eroded down mountains with steep, wrinkled ridges were majestic with the clouds pushed into their summits. The weather was also ideal, warm but not too hot for steady winds blew most all the time. I also found it fascinating that there were no poisonous snakes or dangerous animals in the forests on the islands.

Maeve had previously lived on the other side of the island, the north shore, and we drove over there a couple times to buy some of the "da kine" bud. The marijuana grown on these islands was very potent, very expensive too at $500 an ounce. She had friends over there with names like Big Wave Dave, the guy who dealt us the dope. Most of the people over their were surfer dudes for it was a Mecca for surfers due to the enormous waves that that crossed the Pacific to hit the island there at the north shore.

On one of our trips to the north shore it was night and as we drove across the pineapple fields we saw something in the sky near the mountains off away from the road. It was a ball of fire that crept slowly across the sky, almost like those round Chinese type kites only it was on fire. Maeve commented that it was a comet for it looked like those Medieval paintings that depict comets with flickering flames running off their tails. I told her that it wasn't, for comets are far off in space and stationary to the naked eye; this thing was moving between us and the darkness of the mountains in the background. We observed it a little longer then she commented that there were all sorts of military things going on over that way. We got back in the car and continued on our drive. A few days later I saw a book in the Robbins' library about ghosts and supernatural occurrences on Hawaii. In it, there was a chapter about this strange phenomenon of fireballs. Surely, we had witnessed one for ourselves!

My stay went great and I traded some of my paintings to my hosts for their kindness and hospitality. The fling with Maeve was like a blind honeymoon, but she was far more enthralled with me than I with her; consequently, it all came to a sudden end when one day she asked me if I was in love with her. I told her that I wasn't. I headed back to Boston on the plane and went back living in my new house sharing situation.

I had nothing going on there and I became depressed. I had come to dislike the colder wintry weather for it kept me inside too much. The house I was living in was lousy for painting because the light was so bad; plus, I didn't have enough space to work in. I went walking around in Harvard Square and places, feeling like an outsider to society. Everyone had agendas, classes to attend, jobs to go to, and families to go home to. I saw many beautiful women around and I wondered how it would ever be that I could attract one to have as a partner if I was this aloof, financially insecure, transient loner. Although I did want a woman and a family, I resigned myself to a life where painting was my priority and my commitment. I enjoyed my freedom even if it was very lonely at times. My course as an artist was more like that of a monk who had turned away from the world. Though I longed for love and a family, I had whittled away at my own wants and therefore was content without these things.

The personal needs of each of us is like a fire that consumes things, perpetuating itself and growing as more things are added. It is not recognized by many today that the world is disintegrating; that our planet will not be able to handle ten billion little fires. We are responsible, particularly in the more "developed" countries like our own, for a huge amount of pollution and consummation of raw materials. One American goes through what about what fifty Indians go through in their lifetimes. The hard fact is, is that our species, born yesterday from the killer ape, has ruined the planet in a very short time due to the wants and needs of the ever increasing numbers of individuals that have to share the planet. People really haven't a clue of what they're in for in the near future.

Granted I didn't have a family, but my brother Chris did, and that winter he got into some more trouble due to his ongoing bout with alcoholism. He was arrested late one Sunday evening for drunk driving and it was his second offense within a ten year period so it carried a stiffer penalty. I went out to their house that week and his wife, Fanny, said that he was now living at the neighbor's. I mentioned to her that he had to stop drinking. She seemed unconcerned about that but told me that she wanted a divorce, that she was tired of being Chris's mother ever since they were together. I went over and found Chris. He was very depressed and told me that he had not been drinking since the arrest. This was a lie for I could smell alcohol on his breath. He was frightened of being separated from his two children, for up to this point, he had done most of the child rearing since Fanny had a busy job as a corporate lawyer, working very long hours.

After his court appearance, he was sent to a mandatory in-patient alcohol rehab for two weeks in Framingham. While he was in there, I took over his job for him. He was the sole employee, during the winter months, at a hay farm in nearby Ipswich. The chores were delivering hay and feeds to local customers for their horses. I saw how this mundane job could contribute to his unhappiness.

Once out of the rehab, Chris had a new face and he condemned his former behavior, blaming it on alcoholism, adding that it was this disease that made him marry someone like Fanny. It had been apparent to some of us from the start, that their marriage wasn't the right thing for they were different and there seemed to be no authentic love between them. However, they now had two little toddlers between them. Fanny sold their house, since she was the one with the money, and bought a new smaller one. Chris saw his kids only a few times a week over at her house. Incredibly, within a year they would be back together and she pregnant with another baby!

I found myself a girlfriend that summer while attending a party in Brookline. Her name was Wendy, a reserved, smart, Jewish woman two years older than I was. We had fun for a couple of months and I brought her up to Maine where she met some of my family. Unfortunately, our differences outweighed our similarities. She was childless and in her late thirties. She wanted to get married and have kids with me. The feelings weren't mutual and I was not in love with her, so we broke up.

I am not a person who has been able to play along in a relationship just for the convenience of not being alone. We were unable to continue being friends, but at the end, she told me she wanted to learn how to paint. Having spent quite a bit of time that summer with her, I didn't make all that many paintings, so I didn't earn that much money. By December, I had gone through all my earnings and the prospects of spending another long winter there in that dreary house in Cambridge with a roommate wasn't appealing to me. I had no particular reason to be there, no job or anything. I was restless and wanted to go somewhere else, somewhere warm; but I couldn't, for I didn't have any money.

4

Costa Rica

I went to Costa Rica with a girl named Olivia Cabot. She was a summer person at North Haven and had mentioned in the summer that she wanted to go to Costa Rica, if she could find some people to go with. She had a distant crush on me for quite some time. I called her up from Cambridge, telling her that I wanted to go to Central America to paint, but I that I was entirely broke. Olivia, five years younger than I, is rich by inheritance, a sweet girl but quite spoiled and a little lost. I didn't know her all that well, although my Uncle was hers too, for my Dad's brother married into the Cabot family. Uncle Henry lived over in Cabotville on North Haven, near where Olivia's house was. She told me on the phone that she wanted to buy some paintings from me, so I got her to buy me a ticket in exchange for a painting of equitable value. I informed her that I didn't have any money, that I wasn't a benefactor of a wealthy family as she was. She found this hard to believe, knowing that my family had simply given away Burnt Island as though it was something extra and unnecessary. I told her that if I were to go to Costa Rica with her, that I would need to sell more of my paintings to her in order to earn money to pay my way. She agreed that she would most likely buy more, enjoying the idea that I would have to depend on her for something. I gave up my apartment in Cambridge and flew to Costa Rica with Olivia.

Right from the start, on the airplane, I knew I was in for an unpleasant experience with Olivia. She was rather rude to the stewardess when asked what kind of meal she wanted. "Would you like chicken or fish?" the stewardess politely asked her.

"Neither!" Olivia snarled back at her. Later when we landed in San Jose, we missed the last bus for our destination, so we had to spend the night there in the city. I found a youth hostel that was cheap but rather unpleasant. We could have rented a car or stayed at a hotel. She could afford these things. I couldn't. For her, all this stuff we were doing was new, seeing what it was like being poor. She brought way too much stuff with her: a big duffle bag filled on the bottom with tons of magic markers, colored pencils and acrylic paint tubes. She had way too many clothes as well, and she wound up leaving half her load at the hostel to a gladdened recipient employee. Since I brought lots of art supplies, she did too; only she never did use them.

The next morning I found the bus stop and left her there for a while as I walked around in the city. When I returned with drinks for the both of us, I saw her sitting there with this deadpan stare into the wall in front of her. Without saying anything, she chose one of the drinks that I held in each hand. Commenting on the bus ride ahead, she said, "We'll probably have to sit like this (she feigns scrunching her shoulders together) no matter who you are!"

"You mean you're different because you have lots of money?" I said back and she smiled with a smug sort of grin. She was different, but not in a way that was better.

The bus ride went on and many stops were made. It did get crowded and it made me think of how it was that Olivia, there alone, was worth more money than all of us loaded onto the bus. I kept looking out the window to avoid her weighted stare, thinking of the strange scenario I found myself in: stuck with this childish rich girl who's in love with me, with whom I have to live with for the upcoming weeks if I wished to sell any paintings to her to earn some money.

We got to our destination, a hotel on a hillside of a lake called Arenal. I vaguely knew the owner, Virginia, another summer person from North Haven. She was another benefactor of a wealthy family and, consequently, had bought up land in Costa Rica where her husband built a hotel that catered to the windsurfing that goes on at the forever windy lake. Windmills dotted the hilltops to tap into this power for electricity. Olivia and I split the costs of the room but it was still too expensive there for me. Virginia's husband was a builder and he designed the building with columns like those at Knossos in ancient Crete. An active volcano, Arenal, could be seen in the distance at the far end of the lake. We were going to start out there at Virginia's and play it from there. Though we shared a bedroom, I wasn't interested in sleeping with her. Since I was not interested in getting intimate with her, she became frustrated and it made the next week disastrous.

Olivia was a windsurfer of sorts and I wanted to paint the vicinity. I painted little scenes around the hotel and Olivia went down to the lake to learn how to windsurf. Virginia came by and watched me paint. "Why don't you go down and try windsurfing?" she asked me.

"I'm just going to paint. I can't afford to do that anyway," I said to her knowing that it was $80 a day to rent them.

"Olivia's taking lessons. Why don't you?"

"Olivia can do whatever she wants because she is rich," I said as I continued to paint the little oil painting. Virginia watched over my shoulder. "You know your mother has bought a couple of my paintings," I informed her. She was surprised. I told her that I had very little money and that I needed to earn more by selling some of my paintings. This was sort of why I had made this trek with Olivia.

"Didn't you get money from your family?" she asked.

"No I didn't." She was incredulous of this, for all summer people at North Haven were benefactors of wealthy families. I stopped painting and turned around. "And I only have $600 right now, so I need to find a cheaper rental, or I'll be out of money very soon."

"Well, I won't bother you anymore," she said. "Come up and see our house later if you'd like."

"Sure! Where is it?"

"It's up on the hill near the end of the driveway."

"Okay," I said and she left me so I could finish up my painting. Later, I walked up to check out their house and Virginia showed me around the house that her husband built to house their family of three children. Her partner was off working in San Jose on his latest project. She mentioned that he just came home on weekends.

"So is Olivia your girlfriend?" she beamed as we walked around house.

"No, she's not. I don't know her very well. We're just traveling together." I explained again to her how I was with Olivia in hopes of getting her patronage. I divulged as well that I already knew my trip was going to be hampered by Olivia's spoiled antics. She didn't know Olivia at all, for there was a bit of an age difference; however, she later learned that she and Olivia shared the same godmother.

Back at our room the frustrations mounted for Olivia still wanted to get intimate with me. She went into the bathroom and showered. I went out on the stoop and listened to the howling groans of howler monkeys that came out of the forest, giving her time to clean and change her clothes. Once done, she came out and I went in to take a bath. While the tub was filling up, the door opened and in tip toed Olivia, naked.

"What are you doing?" I asked her from in the tub.

"I want to take a bath with you."

"But you just took a shower! I'm getting out."

"Could you leave the water in, I want to lie in your water."

As I got out to grab a towel, she examined my body with her bulging eyes that looked like black buttons; then she crawled into the tub filled with my dirty water. I went back outside, wandered around, trying to figure out how I could get out of this thing with her. When I came back in she was lying on her bed, staring at the ceiling. I quietly started to read a book I had brought with me. "I don't like to read!" she told me. I didn't respond and kept reading. "Why don't you like me?"

I stopped reading, having to answer her. "I do like you, Olivia. I'm just not interested in getting intimate with you."

"Why not, are you gay?"

"Look, you just don't turn me on alright!" I said and went back to reading my book.

After silently surveying the ceiling for about ten minutes, she said again, "Why don't you like me?"

"Oh brother!" I sighed. "Will you stop?" I knew that she was sort of in love with me, and that if I wanted to, I could play along with her and use her for her money; but I wasn't that type of person. I couldn't be so phony like that with someone.

The next morning we had breakfast together then she went down to the lake to windsurf. I kept painting up near the hotel. She returned early and found where I was, so she stood there behind me and watched me paint, asking me questions constantly. She kept rambling on about things. I was trying to concentrate on my work. I understood that she had, to a certain degree, some mental problems for she was a thirty year old with the mentality of a young teen. She admitted this as well, saying that she felt as though she had never grown up. She had no reason to enter the world like most of us because her inherited wealth had blocked her from the need to work at a job; consequently, she was this spoiled girl who mulled away at her own misgivings. Her behavior gave me even more insight into this strange poverty that seems almost inherent in so many rich kids that I've met.

Later that day, Olivia made a scene down at the lake. She became frustrated at trying to windsurf and she displayed her childish antics by screaming at her instructor. When she came back to the hotel she looked sad and asked me to give her a hug. I did; then she pushed me off her and said, "That's no hug!" and stormed out of the room slamming the door behind her. I went out into the lobby and I saw Virginia there. She told me that the instructor wasn't interested into teaching Olivia anymore, due to her rudeness. I told her about what had just happened.

"Oh god! Where did she go?" she said. Presumably, Olivia went walking around in the dark and when she came back she seemed fully composed with a little smug smile on her face.

I soon found myself a cheaper place to stay, and Olivia retreated back to the United States. Fortunately, I was able to earn a little more money there by doing a commissioned painting of Virginia's hotel. After a month in the region around Lake Arenal, I set off to explore more of Costa Rica.

I went on a bus to Monteverde, a cloud forest wildlife reserve. The trip wasn't all that distant but it took a while on those winding dusty roads. The bus became filled with dust at times and many passengers covered their mouths with cloths. I felt sorry for the bus driver, having to do this each day; but he seemed happy, his bushy mustache helped filter the dusty air. I noticed there to be happy faces on the people in general, unlike the long and disgruntled look on those who I saw commuting to their jobs back in Boston. The people here were poor and it seemed that less was required for their own happiness. We got to the end of the journey and the bus stopped as people requested. I had no agenda or reservations so I followed some other tourists and got a room at a little Inn halfway up the mountain. The next day I found a cheaper place down in the valley, in Santa Elena.

Carrying my canvas and art supplies, I walked up to the mountain park known as the cloud forest because of its constant cloudiness up there at the summit. It was noticeably cooler as I ascended the mountain road, looking for a scene to paint amongst the dense tall trees that were filled with birds and animals. I did a few paintings in this area and got food poisoning or something as well, leaving me bed ridden for a couple days. I could hear out my window a parrot that someone had as a pet and often it moaned and groaned, imitating a woman who was getting fucked. The sultry climate made for a sensual atmosphere. There were definitely plenty of beautiful women there as well.

The next place I went was to Quepos on the Pacific coast. It was intensely hot there, even the ocean was hot. I tried painting early in the mornings when it wasn't so bad. The rest of the time I went to nearby Manuel Antonio on a bus to a beach where squirrel monkeys came right down out of the trees looking for handouts of banana. I rented a very cheap room which had in the attic above my room, and many bats. At dusk, I could hear them clambering to get outside, first a little trickle then an all out exodus. They awoke me, the same way, in the morning during their commute home.

I left Quepos after a couple weeks and went back to San Jose which was a lot cooler, being up at a higher altitude. I also wanted more social interaction, to see more of these beautiful girls walking around. I rented a nicer place than the other rentals I had so far. This one was clean with a nice atmosphere and a free breakfast in a courtyard that was filled with plants. I did just one oil painting in the city, a scene that looked down onto a soccer field. Houses amongst lush vegetation bordered the field and beyond that were mountains, volcanoes that had their summits in the clouds. The rest of the time I wandered about, walking through the streets and parks and eventually into the hotels that had casinos. I knew gambling was a dangerous venture for me, but I was a sucker for it and I was in need of more money so I played Blackjack.

I gambled at a couple different casinos and I won for a change. One casino was in an expensive hotel, a place where prostitutes freely plied their trade. Prostitution was legal in Costa Rica and these women of various ages flaunted their stuff around a bar on the ground floor of the hotel. The casino was here too and some of the girls would parade around the tables looking for business. It wasn't a good place to gamble because their tended to be drunken beginners playing and they could mess up, resulting in lost hands for everyone at the table. I liked watching the girls in there but I played Blackjack more frequently at the other casino which had more tables, more serious players and they screened out prostitutes from loitering in there. I only had $300 left and I chanced a good portion of it in my wagering to eventually come out ahead, winning $800 over a period of a few days. I was tempted to keep playing, but I knew better for surely I would lose it.

My plane ticket left back to Boston soon but I wanted to stay and I could, now that I had more money, so I changed my ticket to return three weeks later. I wanted to learn Spanish and I found a school that was in San Jose. I had enough money to pay for a two week course that included a homestay with a Tico family. Tico is an informal term used for Costa Ricans. I went to classes during the day then I lived with this Spanish speaking family at night. It was a good way to learn Spanish for I had to learn it to communicate at all with them.

After paying the school for my classes and the homestay, I was picked up at my hotel by a driver who worked for the school. His name was Lionel and he helped me load my heavy seabag into the trunk of his red cab and off we went.

"Where are we going?" I asked him.

"To the family you are going to live with."

"I mean, where do they live?"

"In Sabanilla, just a short bus ride from the language academy," he informed me. We drove for about twenty minutes; then we entered a neighborhood of wall-to-wall, one story houses with corrugated tin roofs. We turned down a street where each dwelling had steel grates of vertical bars, making it look almost like a prison block. Halfway down the street, Lionel stopped and honked his horn in rapid succession. Instantly, a young man came out of his house and unlocked the gate to let us in. Lionel introduced me to him. His name was Roy. We went inside and I met Roy's mother and father, Maria and Carlos. Tacky ceramic things hung on the walls of the little abode as did a woven rug that depicted DaVinci's "The Last Supper". It was rather crudely done in tones of orange and black, making it appear that oblong melons rested between each person's shoulders. As Lionel and I sat down at the dinning room table, I told him that I was an artist and I showed him some photos of some of my paintings. He showed them to the others. They were all very intrigued.

"You!" he said with surprise, "did these!"

"Yes. Those are pictures of my paintings," I re-stated. Still bewildered, he started talking to the others in Spanish; none of them spoke any English.

"Samwell." Lionel removed his sunglasses and raised his eyebrows, "could you do a painting for me? I am an Indian." He pointed to himself with one of his thumbs. "I run in marathons and I dress with a headdress…you know, feathers and paint on my face!" I nodded, understanding. "Could you, Samwell, paint me a little painting—he framed in his hands, showing the size he intended—of an Indian running, so I can hang it in my home?"

"Yes, I could do that." What else could I say but that? His eyes popped open wide and he looked at the others with a slight grin. They remained expressionless, not understanding what had just transpired for they didn't understand English. Other friends of the son then entered the house and the small room we were in became quite crowded. Lionel said goodbye and then the parents, Carlos and Maria, showed me my room, a small single bed with a table and lamp next to it. Their bedroom was across the hall and their son Roy's room was next to mine. They were very sincere, gentle, and humble people; but very poor financially. Maria and Carlos looked to be in their sixties, but I was later to learn that he was just fifty and she forty-eight! It was a hard life in poverty that took its toll on their years.

Later that evening we all had dinner together. Carlos said grace first then we ate: black beans, rice and fried plantain. After dinner, we guys played darts out on an open patio area between the shanty houses in the back. A little later, two other sons, Eric and Carlos, came over to the house. Eric, the younger one, had a pregnant wife who was very pretty and Carlos jr. had two young kids. They all talked a while as I sat there on the couch, not understanding anything that was said. The young children stared at me, the stranger, as they veiled their views from behind others' bodies.

After a while I went off with the guys in a car. It was Saturday night and all five of us crammed into a little Pinto and sped off into the night. I hadn't a clue as to where we were going. He drove a little too fast, which seemed to be the way men drove there, slowing down only when the bottom of the car grounded due to our heavy load. After passing through several neighborhoods, we stopped on a deserted street near a bakery. Roy jumped out of the car, went into the store, and came back with a couple loaves of bread. A few blocks later we stopped and we all got out of the car. An elderly woman opened the door to her house and waved her hands at us, welcoming us. We all filed into the house where an old fellow in a turtleneck sweater sat in a chair. Even though we were close to the equator, it did get surprisingly cool at night in these higher altitudes. They all kissed the old guy and they introduced me as their guest from the Language Academy. A football (soccer) game was on the TV so I sat on the couch and watched it while they all talked. After a while the old man, curious of my presence, asked me with slurred speech in English where I came from.

"The United States." I said back to him.

"Which part?" he added.

"Maine," I told him. He looked bewildered. "The East Coast," I said a little louder, noticing his hearing was impaired. He stared at me blankly with his jaw dropped like it was too heavy for him. I noticed on their walls they had three completed puzzles that had been framed. They were photographs of landscapes that had been turned into puzzles. One was a mountain scene that looked like the Rockies; the other was of a river; and next was of a lighthouse that was definitely somewhere in Maine. "I live there!" I told them, pointing to the lighthouse. They all examined it with scrutiny. "I live near there." I added so as to not confuse them that that was my house! The old man nodded his affirmation and they went on talking.

After fifteen minutes we all went into the kitchen to play cards on the kitchen table. We didn't play for money but we all got thirty chips. Twenty-one was the game with some added rules of their own. The wife, who I learned was Carlos's sister, continually made snacks and sandwiches for us. No alcohol was served. After a couple hours, Carlos, the dad won all the chips. It was around midnight then we all left. Back at the house I slept well in the narrow little bed in my room.

The next morning I went to church with Carlos and Maria. I was raised a Catholic, but rarely did I still go to church. I went in this case as a token of friendship to assimilate with them. At Mass one stands and sits often and I noticed that while standing, I was one of the tallest people in there. I am less than six feet tall and never thought myself to be tall; but I was here, amongst these people of mixed Indian and Spanish heritage. I didn't understand much of anything that was said aside from a few words like "El Senior", their name for God. I was starting the Spanish class the next day and I wanted dearly to learn how to communicate in Spanish. Being a type of student again was kind of fun; I was far more mature than as a teenager, when learning anything seemed to be counteractive.

On Monday morning I took the bus into San Jose and attended the classes. It was filled with mostly European women. I took a little oral test to gage my level in the language then I was put into a class with just two other people. Our teacher, Cindy, was a perky Tica in her early twenties. She jokingly complained that she had a "gringo name." No English was spoken in her class, causing us to often thumb through our dictionaries in frustration. After a few days it became easier for I memorized many verbs and learned how to put sentences together. The classes were three hours each morning then three more after lunch. Once out for the day, I walked around, looking at all the beautiful women then boarded the bus back to Sabanilla, the neighborhood where I lived with the family. Once I got off the bus I walked along the street that looked out over the tin roofs of the low houses that covered the residential area like a rusted quilt of reds and grays.

I went to the classes all week then decided to get a hotel room away from the house for Saturday night for I wanted to find a woman. I got a hotel room in the Plaza of San Jose and then wandered around into other hotels' casinos, gambling and watching scores of women who paraded around looking for johns who pay for sex.

Gringos fed this trade. There seemed almost a stereotype of middle aged North American men with pot bellies and balding heads that sported long hair tied into ponytails. They often had young Tica girlfriends in their twenties or even late teens! Most of these guys seemed to be kind of loafers who had moved to Costa Rica where they now were rich in this relatively poor country. I had seen on other occasions, old white guys in their fifties and sixties with young brown skinned Tica wives and their little children.

While playing Blackjack in a hotel's casino, I spotted this beautiful long haired, stacked woman across the room. I noticed her looking at me so I cashed in what chips I had won and went over to talk to her. She wore tight, white cotton knee pants and a blue tube top that exposed her smooth shoulders and deep cleavage. "Are you looking for company?" she asked me in English.

"Yes I am. How much?" I asked in Spanish. She told me and I agreed that I wanted to take her back to my hotel room at another hotel just blocks away. Once outside she grabbed my arm to be led and many taxis stopped, hoping that we needed a lift, causing a cacophony of honking horns because of the blocked traffic. Further down the block a ragged homeless woman came up to me and tugged on me free arm, begging for some money. I reached into my pocket and came up with a mil colone bill and gave it her. She examined it with wide opened eyes. My purchased date laughed at the situation. Her name was Sandra, a Colombian woman who lived part-time in Costa Rica to earn money which she brought back home to her family. She was truly stunning, I thought, with her womanly form, poise and femininity.

At my hotel she had to sign in at the desk and they checked her ID, knowing her to be the working woman she was. We took the elevator up which was operated by an old guy who melted in his stance as he gazed at her beautiful breasts. She smiled and winked at me, holding my hand and making little circles in my palm with her ring finger. Once in the room, I started to rub her breasts. As we started to take our clothes off she asked me how old I was. "Guess." I said. She examined my naked body up and down and then guessed thirty. "I have thirty-six." I said in Spanish.

"Guess for me?" she said with a big smile.

"Thirty."

"Right!" she said with surprise and she hugged me softly, her heaving tits pressed into my chest and I could feel her nipples hardening, causing me to get an erection. I bent down and sucked each nipple. Her hands pressed the back of my head into her full, firm bosoms; then she pushed me back and told me to lie down on the bed. Reaching into her bag, she got a bottle of coconut oil and poured some on my hard-on and started stroking me. My hands rubbed her silky thighs then slid into her wet pussy. She climbed up to straddle my midsection, hovering over me. In a circular motion she dragged her breasts over my cock. I held it between them. "Push them together!" she said frantically then she pumped up and down. I soon came, squirting my load mostly onto my chest with some drops hitting my face. She examined my mess with excited interest, slapping her hand playfully in the little puddle; then she laughed-her job complete. I walked her back over to the place where I found her, and then I returned to my hotel room.

The next morning I went back to Sabanilla and I painted the little painting that Lionel had requested. He had dropped off some photos of himself running in his Indian garb, so I used one to make a painting of. Out in their back patio I stretched a little canvas over a small piece of plywood and I did the little oil painting in about three hours-it was Lionel running with his headdress and some mountains in the background. I showed it to Carlos and Maria and they were stunned that I was capable of doing such a thing.

By the end of the second week I could communicate much better with my hosts. One day Carlos told me that Maria had something for me and she approached me with her head down and held out a 2,000 colone bill. I had left it in a pocket of my trousers that she had washed.

At the end of the week, I ran into Lionel at the school and I told him that I had completed his painting. At first he forgot who I was and then he remembered me. I told him that I wanted 10,000 colones for it (one tenth the amount I would charge back in the States) "Oh no!" he uttered and his face saddened.

"Well how much were you expecting to pay me for it?" I asked him. He held his chin in silence. I realized then that he hadn't been expecting to pay anything. "I'll tell you what...you give 5,000 colones to my family for your painting."

Now he spoke. "I give 5,000 colones to the family for your painting...money you give them as a gift?"

"Yes," I said and we shook hands. He came over later and got the painting, saying that he liked it very much and that he would proudly display it in his house, adding that he didn't have the money but would give it to them later. I don't think he ever paid them or that they wanted him to pay them because what I did was just too weird a thing.

The school finished and so was my homestay. I learned quite a bit of Spanish only now it was time to return on my plane ticket back to Boston, where I wouldn't be speaking any Spanish. It was late March and I didn't have anywhere to stay. From the airport in Boston I took the subway to North Station then a train to the North Shore where I had left my car at a friend's house. I continued driving up to Maine, to Portland where I rented a room for a week in cheap hotel with my dwindling savings. I walked around, checking out Portland, going to the library and reading things, seeing if it was a place where I could live next. I didn't like it very there there very much. Maybe the sterile grayness of March contrasted against the vibrant tropics made it gloomier for me; also, the homogeneous social scene there of nothing but white people, was something that I didn't like. Compounded by the fact that I had no money left, I felt displaced and not belonging, nothing that was new to me.

With $80 left, I drove to Rockland and took the ferry out to North Haven where I braved the cold, staying in our house. Of course there was no water on yet, nor did I have heat, but it was free there. I just dressed heavily in layers and was snug under several blankets at night. Little winter diving ducks that aren't seen in the Summer were frolicking in the ocean just in front of the house at high tide. I could see bufflehead, mergansers, and goldeneye as well, so I did little studies of them. I had plenty of time and solitude and space to paint, so I did.

My ability to paint stemmed from the inordinate amount of time I spent alone in my life. At times like these in Maine, I would go days or even weeks without even talking to another soul. The organic nature of creativity itself is like an ever changing river flowing downstream, forced by the water upstream. I am compelled to paint because of who I am and the identity engrained in each piece that make. Yet to say that they are all mine and for me would be wrong, for like myself and us as human beings, we have an ancient past and we are only the latest in an unbreakable string of events that have brought us here. To think that I am my own and these my paintings is analogous to thinking that the water one sees coming out of a faucet is of that faucet, when obviously, it has an endless history of coming through the pipes and water mains, the reservoirs and aquifers, the rain, etc. What I do is simply the latest in a saga that stretches deep into the past. I paint not only for myself, but the identity of all of us. This is what I think true art is all about.

After a few weeks I called my sister Dinah who lived in California with her husband and kids. She informed me that Dad had a cancerous tumor that blocked his esophagus.

"Dad has cancer!" I said with surprise.

"He doesn't have cancer. He has a cancerous tumor." She spoke with a tone of denial.

"That's what cancer is! Is it malignant?"

"I'm not sure. He has the best doctors around and he's been taking medicines to shrink them. He's going in for more tests tomorrow."

"I'm at North Haven!" I told her and I explained briefly my last couple of months.

"It must be freezing!" she said. "Is the water on already?"

"No. I'll have to wait quite a bit longer because it's still freezes at night. I flush the toilet with a bucket of ocean water and I get my drinking water by driving to a well mid island. I've even showered by standing under overflowing gutters when it rains."

"Oh my God! Sam, are you alright?"

"Yeah, I'm fine. I'm getting lots of painting done and the warmer weather's just around the corner."

"Do you need anything?"

"Yes. I'm totally broke. Can I borrow some money?"

"Well I can loan you $200. I know you'll have money this summer or I'll buy one that you've done."

"Thanks Dinah!" I said with relief. "Can you not tell Dad that I'm here? You know that I'm not allowed to be here."

"I won't tell him. I'm glad somebody's there using our house!" His policies had become more and more restrictive, even to them too. He had been getting renters for August to keep all his children away.

Spring comes late to Maine and even later out on these islands because of the frigid ocean. By June it warmed up and I called my father to tell him I was there at his house. Surprisingly, he told me to take good care of the house for one day it would be mine. This revealed a change in him for the year prior I thought that most likely he would be leaving that house to his wife Wendy. He told me how he was taking chemotherapy and that most likely he wouldn't make it to Maine that summer. I told him that I was sorry that he had to go through all of this. I later sent him a poem or quote from Rumi, a Persian poet who I admired, throwing it his way in hopes that he might understand it, and that it would help him.

THE WORLD IS THE SEA, THE BODY A FISH AND THE SPIRIT JONAH, KEPT FROM THE LIGHT OF DAWN. IF THE SPIRIT IS FILLED WITH GLORIFYING GOD IT IS DELIVERED FROM THE FISH; OTHERWISE IT IS DIGESTED AND DISAPPEARS.

The sickness my father had was brought about by his own actions of boozing for fifty years. As I understood it though, it was a disease. It is portrayed in AA as a three headed monster (physical, emotional, and spiritual). It was there in my father for me to see in all its facets. I hoped that his sickness would change his heart.

My brother George came up from New York in early July. He looked better than he had the last time I had seen him when he was terribly gaunt and underweight. He had suffered from colitis earlier, and was now in better health for he had changed to a vegan diet. Despite our mutual intentions to close the gap that had grown between us, he did something to me that undermined my trust with him. When he called Dad to wish him a happy birthday, he left a message that he was calling from North Haven. Later when Dad called back George was upstairs and we simultaneously picked up the phones. Dad asked George to make sure the house was clean before the renters arrived, adding that I was to help. Before I had a chance to say anything, George goes, "I don't know about that!"

"What do you mean, won't Sam help you?"

"Humph. I've pretty much learned not to rely on Sam for anything at this point!" he said smugly. My brother's back-stabbing nature was obviously still there. Angry hearing this, Dad asked him to get me. George hollered from upstairs that Dad was on the phone. I started talking, George hung up.

"Of course I'll clean up the house for the renters. I'll try to get George to help me!" I emphasized. I told him of other things that I had done around the house, fixing things that had experienced years of neglect.

"Atta boy, Sammy!" he said and our conversation was over. I didn't mention to George that I had heard him until his last day there.

"You must think that I don't help around here," I told him.

"Why's that?"

"Because that's what you told Dad," I said to him and his head became stilled.

"No. I told him that we were both going to help clean the house for the renters."

"I picked up the phone the same time you did and I heard what you said."

As though he was a balloon that had been deflated, he withered in his stance. His eyes bulged out and, as he looked at me, the cathartic cry of a young child came out of him. "Just give me a hug and tell me that you love me!"

"No! Why do you do things like that to me?"

"I don't mean to—I mean sometimes I just do!" he said sobbing away.

"And this book you're writing about me. You're so full of shit."

"Fuck you!" he said, instantly changing his expression into a fully composed sinister one. I found his swaying demeanor spooky and psychotic, so I refrained from any further remarks and walked out of the room. A little later when he was leaving, on his way to the ferry, he said, "You'll clean up for them, right!"

The usual crowds came in August. My sisters Eliza and Susan came up from New York for a couple weeks. While out on a picnic with them, I learned that Susan was writing a new book called, <u>My Life with No One</u>. She divulged that it was about a male artist who lives a wandering existence, painting to find his soul. This was about me again! Like George, she was using the various stories that I had told her about my life. Eliza was a writer too and she had just returned from a winter's stay, under the sponsorship of some rich friends, in Bali and had completed her first novel, <u>The Tiny One</u>. It was accounts of herself as a child, arranged around the day our mom died. She was only seven then, but she boosted her character's age to nine. She was getting published with Knopf, as were Susan and George. Eliza had George's agent and Susan's editor.

5

The Coral Route

I continued traveling and painting that winter, going first back to Hawaii where I there planned the rest of my trip. I bought a plane ticket from Newark to Hawaii at a travel agency in Rockland; then headed out from New York in early November just as the cold wintry air was setting in. I stayed at the Robbins' again and when I arrived they asked me what my plans were. I hadn't any. Hoping to find something wonderful in Hawaii, like a girl to live with there, I told them that I was heading off in three weeks but avoided giving them a destination for I didn't have one yet. I informed them that my sister Dinah was living with her family in Australia and that I planned on visiting them around Christmas. The next day I went to a travel agency at the Kahala Mall and I asked about plane tickets. The agent told me of Air New Zealand's "Coral Route" ticket that permitted five stops over a period of six months. This was perfect for me, so then and there I picked five stops: Rarotonga, Auckland, Brisbane, Tahiti, and back to Los Angeles. I bought the ticket for $1,350 with $100 bills I carried in my pocket. Now I could give my hosts a firm agenda. They were very welcoming to me for they enjoyed art and seeing how it is that an artist does his thing.

I was able to get a lot of painting done. They had a car that they supplied to guests and I went off each day to make paintings. The first one was done at the base of the Koolaus Cliffs. Steep and tall, they drop off into a flat verdant valley on the Leeward side of Oahu.

I had onlookers while painting. A man of Japanese descent walked up to see what I was doing. He told me that he painted too and he went back to his house to retrieve some photos of his work: paintings of crashing waves, similar to traditional Chinese stuff I had seen-the waves spreading into little fingers. After silently watching me paint for ten minutes, he left then another fellow stopped on his motorcycle. He told me that he wanted to buy it! He said he had a ranch right nearby and he gave me his card with his phone number on it. I never called him back for I wasn't in need of selling it since I had plenty of money in the bank from earlier sales that summer. Next some Hawaiian locals pulled alongside me in their car, giving me the "thumbs up" in their approval of my painting.

Another day I painted up at a scenic lookout on a highway just before it enters a long tunnel that cuts deeply through the mountain. From this spot I was able to paint a scene that included the sacred mountain of Ola Mauna, pointed up in a triangle with the blue ocean behind it. Others included one further along the coast-a seascape from the beach looking across the bay to an island called Chinaman's Hat. This spot was right on the coastal busy road so many people stopped to see what I was doing. Some of them want to talk and ask me questions, but I remain as quiet as possible so they'll continue on. One blonde woman stopped in her car, got out and said hello, telling me she painted too. She stood behind me and said, "I like it!" I kept working, looking back to see her smiling. She left after a little and I felt that I had just blown a chance for a date, for I was too wrapped up in my painting to give her any attention.

My hosts, the Robbins, were very busy each day working at the law firm and each evening I gave them a display of what I had most recently painted. Sometimes I had dinner with them and we talked. Ken told me that his son, Tim, lived on the island and that Tim was about to go into the Air Force. I mentioned that I had been in the military, in the Navy as a Seabee. Ken was surprised and he told me that he had been an officer in the Navy during Vietnam. "I was in charge of a platoon that patrolled a very dangerous harbor. My guys were sort of riff raff…you know guys who had been to Captain's Mast."

"I went to Captain's Mast too," I quietly mentioned.

"You did?"

"Yes, that's how I got out, by going to Captain's Mast three times. I was UA three times on purpose because I was unable to quit. I definitely wasn't the military type!"

"No. You aren't," he agreed.

"I am glad I did it though. I learned a great deal about human nature and my personal value for freedom." Ken nodded then looked off and changed the subject.

I soon met his son Tim, a 27 year-old who was heading into the military not much unlike the way I had. Ken asked me not to say things to Tim that would make the military seem bad. I didn't, but I could foresee that Tim would have big difficulties fitting in for he was a surfer dude who smoked a good deal of pot. We all played golf together and later Tim took me around in his van and we scored a little bud. I warned him that he could go to prison in the military for failing the urinalysis tests. He felt there were ways to get around it.

I wanted to visit and paint some of the other islands and Shaunagh suggested that I go to the Big Island, Hawaii itself. I told her how I hadn't a credit card so renting a car there would not be possible for me. She soon remembered a friend of hers who lived over there and thought that he might be someone I would like. She contacted her friend, Michael, told him about me, and later reported to me that he would happily rent a car for me and I could pay him with cash. She gave me his phone number and I called him only to get an answering machine. I left a message on it saying when I was arriving at Hilo and that I would be dressed in green clothes so that he could identify me at the airport there. So after my second week at the Robbins' house, I bid them farewell, left a painting as a token of thanks, and headed to the airport.

It was a short plane ride over to the Big Island, a giant cloud covered mountain that poked out of the deep Pacific. When I got off the plane at Hilo, a misty rain fell so fine that some minute droplets floated upwards. I saw a low arching bright rainbow, greeting me as I walked outside from the parked plane to the terminal and baggage claim area. I got to the single baggage area and waited. The baggage carousel alarmed and the conveyor-belt started to move. I looked around for a man who might be looking for me but I hadn't worn green like I had told him I would. I did where a green T shirt but I had blue jeans on. My two items came out early. I picked them up and decided to go over to the car rental area to wait there. After a few moments, a bearded fiftyish, slight built fellow came around a corner, looking inquisitively at me.

"Are you Michael?"

He held out his hand and greeted me. "You're not dressed in green!" I shrugged my shoulders. "So how long would you like to rent a car?"

"Until Tuesday," I told him. It was Friday, Friday the 13th of November and my plane flight to Rarotonga left from Honolulu the coming Tuesday evening.

He conversed with the rental agent and got the car for me, then told me that he had to go to work. He offered that I could stay at his house with him, or that I could go to one of the bed and breakfasts that were advertised in his magazine. He mentioned that a woman had come with him who was interested in seeing what an artist does. With a turn of his head, he nodded towards a blonde woman in an orange and white pullover dress. She was walking on the sidewalk in a slow steadied way that made it seem like she was floating along. "This is Johanna and she's a neighbor," Michael said. I shook her hand. She silently shrugged her shoulders and smiled fully at me. "She was looking for you but you aren't dressed in green." He grinned and patted me on the shoulder. "So what do you want do?"

"I guess I'll start by staying with you at your house."

"Do you want to take her with you?"

"Sure, that's fine!" I said, looking at her standing there with a slight smile.

"Good. We'll see you later tonight. I have to go back to work." She hugged him and gave him a little kiss. A smile appeared on his tired face. I put my stuff into the trunk of the rented car and off I went with Johanna.

"This is my first time here," I told her as we drove out of the parking lot. "I'm a painter and I want to get as many paintings done as I can while I'm here."

"I know," she said softly like it was to herself. I detected a bit of a European accent but she didn't say anything else. She had a pleasant demeanor, like she was happy, seeming to be on the verge of breaking into laughter. "You can go dis way." She pointed for me to change roads.

We stopped and picked up some refreshments for the trip, an hour or so drive to the southern tip of the island. I learned that she was from Finland but had lived many places in her thirty years and had been there on the Big Island for two now. Ready to leave the island now, she claimed that she was bored. I chomped into a Fuji apple I had just bought, devouring rather swiftly, being thirsty from the flight.

"You're hungry!" she said with a big smile. "Do you smoke?"

"No I don't."

"Do you mind if I smoke?"

"No," I said and added, "I don't smoke cigarettes but I have a little pot. Want to smoke some?"

"Sure!" she beamed.

I reached into my pocket and came out with a mini zip-loc bag that contained the small bud that I had bought back in Honolulu with Tim. While driving, I manufactured a pipe from an aluminum can just emptied of its contents and we each took a couple of hits. She told me she had other names and she reeled them off. They were Indian ones. She had spent some years living in India and had learned the Hindi language.

"What other languages do you speak?" I asked.

"I can speak a little German too. And Finish of course, but nobody speaks Finnish anywhere except in Finland. Even the Swedes and Norwegians can understand each other's language, but ours is different."

The road climbed at a very subtle angle but continued up high so that now the terrain was not tropical anymore, more like a baron part of New England with dry shrub trees. "It's quite cold up here. I'm surprised," I said as I rolled up my window.

"Yes." She smiled brilliantly and faced me in her seat, digging her sky blue eyes at me in a stare as I drove. I told her more about myself: that I currently didn't live anywhere; that I was on the first leg of a journey, a winter tour to the South Pacific, New Zealand, and Australia. I added that I had spent half the year on an island in Maine where I earned enough money from sales of paintings to sponsor myself this tour to keep painting where I go. "Dat's wonderful!" she said. "What a great way ta live!" She proceeded to tell me how many places she had lived since leaving Finland at eighteen: Japan, Hong Kong, Thailand, Sri Lanka, India, Bali, Australia and Germany. Hawaii was the only place in the U.S. she had lived. "I've really been here too lung." We sloped down now at a slight angle and up ahead was a spectacular view, one of many that I would see in the next few days. The clouds came in off the ocean and dissipated into the slopes of a massive monadnoc dome shaped mountain.

"Wow! I could paint that!" I mentioned that I might try to paint one that day if I had time. It was already after 3:00 in the afternoon.

"I would like to join you if I can."

"Certainly. After I unload my stuff I can stretch a canvas and we'll go somewhere."

The road kept declining toward the coast in the distant. We were now amongst black volcanic rocks, sharp angular boulders, a wasteland that extended far down to the coast. We drove down into the meandering roads of a greener, wooded area until we reached the driveway where Michael lived. It was a mile or so up a red dirt road to his house. She pointed to the grassy driveway where she stayed as we passed it, turning up past a macadamia grove and other planted trees to where Michael's house was, an elevated A frame with a deck around its perimeter. We walked in and she showed me where I would be sleeping; obviously she was familiar with his house. I unpacked my stuff, quickly stretched a canvas and we returned to the car to go off to find a place to paint.

"Where should we go?" I asked her, not knowing anything about the place where we were. The sun was dropping lower and daylight was running out. "Let's go down to the ocean since it looks pretty close." We passed an area with a dozen windmills harnessing the power of the steady breeze that blows off the water; then we made it to the cliffs that drop down to the ocean which was a marvelous bluish purple color with lighter areas where the strong gusts scored the ocean's surface. Wanting to paint low out of the wind, I chose to do a smaller painting and I brought it out, propped it against a cement pillar that was conveniently there. I squirted out the colors I use and with her watching I did a very fast painting of the seascape there with the sun heading down into a bank of clouds far off at the horizon. I did it in about twenty minutes. "That's beautiful!" she said, then went back into the car to roll herself a cigarette. I cleaned up my brushes, put my stuff back in the car and off we drove back up the sloping hill to where Michael lived. I dropped her off where she told me to stop. "Do you remember which road Michael lives on?"

"Yes. I think I can find it."

"Maybe I'll come up tomorrow." She walked off into a grassy road that led to her place.

I found Michael's house and fumbled around in the dark for a light for he wasn't home yet. There were stacks of paper that lay around on his floors. I put on a tape of some Spanish guitar, started to look at some books he had and then saw some headlights coming up his driveway. It was Michael. He parked his pick up beneath the house, came up and we talked for a little while. He told me that I could take a shower if I wanted but that it was cold water only. I declined his offer and soon went to bed on an air mattress that he had for me on the floor.

The next morning I awoke before he did, tiptoed about silently and made some tea. He came down from his loft and enquired about where I was going to go paint. "I don't know yet. I'll just explore around and find a place." I told him.

"Is Johanna coming with you?" he asked with concern.

"I don't know," I said. At that, sauntering up the road was Johanna. She came in Michael's house and made herself a cup of coffee, made a couple phone calls, then told me that she wanted to come with me. I had a new canvas all ready stretched and we left the house.

We drove around and she was my guide. In an hour or so we reached the Kona Coast, a drier hotter area away from the clouds that hugged the mountain slopes. We poked through the town and kept going. The highway ahead went through another lava field, no trees or anything, just black chunks of newly formed volcanic rock. Once we were over a gradual slope, the view was magnificent. Past the black lava field was a cobalt blue ocean then another huge dome of a mountain. "That's Maui." She informed me.

"I would like to paint here but I don't like standing next to these cars speeding by." We kept driving along this black rock desert. "Maybe we'll just drive around the whole island today," I said to her as she just sat there motionless, looking out the window. Next we came up to a steep hilly grassy area. I stopped the car to look closer at the scene.

"Are you going to paint here?" she said getting a little impatient.

I stepped out of the car and felt a stiff breeze which instantly changed my mind, due to the difficulties of painting in strong winds. "Let's keep going." I said. We stopped at a little mall area at her request, where there was an organic whole foods store. We both got some snacks for lunch. She ran into a man she knew and talked to him for a while as I waited for her in the car. Once back in the car, she pointed to a spot on the map that was a scenic place, so we went there.

After a little more driving we made it to the spot, a lookout park area at the end of one of the roads. I surveyed the area and found a place to paint. We were high on a cliff that overlooked a dramatic coastline where there was a sharp drop off to the ocean below. I had to be quite close to the edge to catch the view of the coast, so I went around a little fence, stood a meter from the precipice and decided to paint there. I ran back up to the car where she was standing and told her I could do it down there, pointing to my chosen spot on the cliff's edge. "Let's smoke a little first," I said. She agreed and we climbed back into the car to take a couple hits off the soda can pipe I had. I gathered my painting stuff together. She carried an item for me and we walked down around the fence to my chosen spot. I opened up my telescoping aluminum easel, squirted out some oil paints onto my palette, and started to paint. "I have to do this kind of quickly because the light in the same scene changes as time passes. I start with the lightest areas first so it doesn't get muddied," I told her as she stood behind me, looking over my shoulder. I did the sky and clouds first. We could see very far away because we were high up and the atmosphere was clear even though rain showers were occurring in little patches. The sun shone through the clouds casting a bright turquoise color on the darker blue shaded areas of the ocean. "I'll have to get that quickly," I said and it already vanished by the time I mixed the colors. "It was sort of like this, right?" I consulted her.

"I don't think it went up that high." She advised me where I should be putting the paint. One of the power pack rain showers now traversed over the ocean in front of us almost obscuring the horizon behind it. The rain that pelted the ocean made discernable shapes that could be seen on the surface through the veils of the showers. "That's so beautiful," she said about scene in front of us. "They're like spirits dancing on the water."

I instantly made an area in the center of the painting to try document this special, ephemeral scene. Then a shower hit us, softly at first, then hard. I pulled my canvas off the easel and we both rushed up to the safety of the car. "Each painting I make has its own story behind it because of the things that happen to me when I do them," I told her as the torrents of rain hit the roof of the car. She giggled a little then finished the second half of a cigarette. The rain soon passed and I went back to paint.

I filled in the canvas. New incredible sights happened in the open space in front of me because of the changeable clouds and the variations of sunlight. I thought about the great number of paintings that could be done from that one spot and how different and original each of them could be; but I only had one for today. The rain started again and we packed up to leave. I put my paints and stuff into the trunk and put my painting in the back seat on a board I found to keep it from touching the rent-a-car's upholstery and we drove off into the pouring rain.

After driving a ways down the road, Johanna peered back to look at my painting. "It is like us: two rain showers." she said to me as I drove.

"Notice how my scene is something that never really happened—I mean it's sort of a combination of stuff we saw that I put down."

"Yes, but your scene is just as real now!" she pointed out. We drove back home going the other way around the island, back towards Hilo. The car fogged up due to the colder rain outside and I asked her to turn on the air conditioner or fan to fix this problem for I was concentrating on driving and was having a hard time seeing through the windshield. "I dunt know how," she said after pushing a couple levers on the dash. She was like me. Machines and modern things were foreign to her for they were of the unnatural world. I was able to open a vent after a while and the windshield cleared up.

Further into the drive I noticed that she held her left hand. She had a deep snake-like scar in her open palm that went from her wrist up to her middle finger. She told me that she had fallen on some glass months earlier and that it still hurt. I asked her if I could hold it. She consented and put her left hand onto my right. Her hand was hot and I moved my thumb over the scar. "Maybe this will help." I said and she stayed silent and still. We listened to the radio and no longer talked but there was a silent communication going on between us. At times she pulled her hand away, changed her seating position then offered her hand back, palm up for me to touch again.

I dropped her off where I had the day before at the grassy road that led to her place. It was dark out and when she opened the car door the light went on in the cab. She sat there with a little smile, looking straight ahead, waiting for me to do something. "It was nice to see you," I said and reached over to kiss her on the cheek but she dodged her head away.

"Nice fa me too," she said, "I'll see you tomorrow." As she got out, a man with a flashlight came out of the darkness. She introduced me to him as I sat inside the car.

"Is that a rent-a-car?" the man asked. "Do you need help getting through the dark Johanna?"

"That would be nice. Good night Sam!" she said and followed the guy down the dark path. I drove back up to Michael's and he was home.

"That was a long day!" he said, greeting me as I walked in. "Did you drop Johanna off?"

"Yeah, she's down there."

"Where did you go?"

"I don't remember the name of the spot but I can show you the painting."

"That would be great!" he said and I went out to the car to fetch my painting. He recognized where I had done it then said, "Nino called for Johanna, wondering if she had returned." I didn't say anything back, not knowing who Nino was. We chatted a bit and he gave me some books to look at. The electricity in his house came from solar panels so only one light was on. He turned another one on for me and informed me that the battery becomes noticeably lower when it's not him alone living there. "Light a fire if you want," he offered. We were up the slope of a mountain where it did get a bit colder but I wasn't cold. He noticed me looking at his magazines so he told me that he had been publishing them for three years now, admitting that it was a losing venture and that he was ready for something different. He told me he went to Cornell and had dodged going to Vietnam by being a language specialist in Japanese. He was obviously an intelligent and progressive fellow, but he seemed quite unhappy with his current life. I went to bed and slept well.

In the morning I was anticipating the return of that girl but by 10 AM she hadn't shown up. I stretched a new canvas and got ready to head out again to paint. "Where are you going today?" Michael asked me.

"I'm not sure."

"I'm sure the day has its own agenda for you!"

"Yes. That's a good way of putting it," I said, agreeing with his observations of my non-planned ventures. I got in my car and drove off. At the bottom of the driveway was Johanna, walking lazily up the dirt road to Michael's. I stopped and told her I was going off to paint.

"I'd like to come," she said to me.

"That's fine! If you don't have anything else to do?" She climbed in and we headed out in the same direction we had the day before. "I'd like to go swimming in the ocean. Do you know a place where we can go?" I asked.

"Yes, I know where we can go." She hadn't been very talkative the day before but now that she was more comfortable with me, she began to tell me more about herself. She had a five year old son who lived on the island, mostly with his dad, a German man who lived on a commune there. They no longer were together and they shared custody but she felt it was better for her son to be at the commune because there were more people there. Knowing that she didn't have any money, I asked what the father did to support his child. "He grows ganja. I have a little with me too if you want to smoke some." She rolled a little joint that had a small crutch or filter made from a piece of matchbook—the same way she rolled her cigarettes. "Did you dream last night?" she asked.

"Yeah, but I don't remember it. Why?"

"I dreamt that I was walking up the road—you know the road near Michael's—and I saw this tiger. It didn't attack me or anything; it just looked at me and crossed the road in front of me and went bock to da woods."

"That's incredible!" I said. Not telling her that another girl had once dreamt of this tiger after we had met. I said, "It was me."

"It was you," she said in a very soft way.

After a while she told me to take a left turn and we made our way down a meandering road to the coast and a small settlement of houses built amidst the black lava fields that seemed almost industrial because the lava resembled broken chunks of asphalt. Reaching the road's end, we parked near a little Hawaiian church where a Sunday service had just ended. Dark skinned Hawaiians dressed in colorful clothes exited their little church house that was painted in bright pastel colors. We took a five minute walk on a path through some gnarly dead trees and some littered garbage, arriving at a little enclave of a beach. Only two other people were there and they sat up under the palms that bordered the beach.

We went for a swim. First I went in and then she followed. I swam around her underwater, opening my eyes, seeing her graceful body tread water. I faintly brushed against her, touching her leg.

We got out and sat on her sarong. As she lay there in her bikini I noticed what a fine woman she was and how special the air of the moment had become. We had bought a newspaper on the way and I read some of it to her. "There's this meteor shower happening early Tuesday morning, the Leonids. Supposedly, there will be hundreds of shooting stars per hour."

"I hope I see it!" she said. "I'm hot. I'm going bock in." She dove in and I followed. This time in the water, I swam up to her and held her in a basket carry in my arms. I slowly twirled her around, looking down into her eyes. Our eyes locked and her face brightened; then she looked away, slowly returning her gaze at me. I leaned down to kiss her but she turned her head away again and smiled. I let her head drop back slowly into the water so that her hair and ears were submerged. She closed her eyes and I stroked her forehead back to her hairline like I was baptizing her.

We got out again and I read more of the paper to her. Her English was pretty good but she had to ask what some words meant as I read. A scruffy little dog came over and sat in the sand about ten feet from us. After a few moments she said, "Look, he wants ta be wid us!" The dog, sandy and hot, was panting uncomfortably but refrained from rejoining its master who sat off down the beach under the shading palms. We both felt that the dog recognized a good thing that we kindled being together.

We left the beach and went back to driving around in the car. The clouds were building up over the land but it remained sunny and clear just off the coast. We stopped in Kona, had some lunch and the day flew by. "Aren't you going to paint today?" she asked me.

"I don't know. I don't have to paint." We found a park area, an old air strip on the coast next to a beach. It was a huge asphalt parking lot with some grass and weeds poking up through cracks. I let her try driving the car there for she had mentioned that she didn't know how to drive—people always drove for her. Her attempt to drive didn't last long because she accelerated much too fast then slammed the brakes, screeching the car to a halt. She laughed and had enough. We sat on the beach, watched the ocean and talked. "What does this mean?" I asked her, pointing to an earring she wore.

"It's Hebrew," she said. "It's the number eighteen. It is—how do you say—a good luck…"

"A good luck charm," I completed for her.

"When I went to Japan, I juss show op there at the airport with nothing ta do and some Israelis were there and they noticed my earring. So I stayed with them at first."

"Then what did you do? Did you work there?"

"Yes, the girl I was with worked at a nightclub. It was the Japanese mafia's, you know, and she was doing too much coke so they took me instead. I made lots of money and had free coke. The men there love blonde women and take very good care of us; but they aren't so nice to their own women." She fiddled with the sand, making little round designs in it with her fingers.

The sun was low now, about to set over the ocean's horizon. We looked back toward the mountain which was encased by clouds and we saw a gigantic double rainbow in a full 180 degree arc. We moved off the beach and sat on a bench that faced inland to view this monstrous rainbow. "This is a good sign," she said and turned to kiss me softly on my lips.

"I see a different rainbow than you," I told her. She looked at me with a bewildered expression. "It's true! You see the shadows of our heads over there on that wall? Your rainbow's center is where your head is, and mine is where my head is." It was evident to see this because of the semi circle of the vivid rainbow. The sun then proceeded to set over the horizon behind us and this majestic rainbow slowly disappeared from the bottom up, like nothing I had ever seen—a massive curtain, slowly being raised to introduce the night. We kissed a little more then returned to the car.

We drove back to where we stayed and this time she invited me to her shack, no electricity or anything, but she said she stayed there for free. It was dark out and she told me to enter from another adjacent road. I stopped and parked the car in the middle of a very narrow road that had tall grass on both sides. "I think I can find it through here." she whispered to me as we fumble in the dark. We then saw a flashlight beaming about, eventually spotting us and blinding our vision. It was the guy she introduced me to a couple days earlier. He was the owner of the land and he escorted us to her shack, inviting himself in. "I'm glad I came out! I noticed someone's headlights through the trees," he said. Johanna looked at me and rolled her eyes. He made himself at home and started rambling on about nonsense that neither of us wanted to hear. Resembling a goat with his long thin beard that dropped just from the point of his chin, he kept talking for fifteen minutes; then another fellow showed up at her shack.

"Hi Nino!" said Johanna.

Suddenly the crackpot landlord got quite upset and he became belligerent. "I don't want all these people on my land and I didn't invite any of you here!"

"Peace brother," Nino said to him. They obviously already had met before.

"And Johanna, I've had it with you! All you do is smoke my pot and you don't do anything around here," he said fuming.

"That's no problem," Johanna said calmly.

"Yeah, everybody out! Now!" he staggered a little, looking for the door.

"I'm sorry Sam," Johanna said to me. "I'll see you tomorrow."

I made my way out to the car, being escorted there by the guy with his flashlight. "Watch out for her man—I'm telling ya! She's a mooch," the drunken fellow warned. I backed my car out the road and returned to Michael's.

"What did you paint today?" Michael asked me when I walked into his house.

"We didn't do one today." He was noticeably stirred. I could tell that he had some feelings for her too. I told him what had just transpired down at her shack and he seemed surprised at his neighbor's behavior. We continued to talk as we had the night before. He asked me if I had any children and I told him that I hadn't any. "I look at all the little ones as my children, all the people around my age—my brothers and sisters, and the older people are my parents." I broadly informed him of my family orientation.

"Yes, I'm sort of that way too. All I really do want though is to have a lasting relationship with a person and a place—something that I haven't been able to find yet!" he told me in such a fashion that it would have been appropriate for him to have been pulling on his hair with both hands. I made my way to bed and tried to sleep but I couldn't very well.

In the morning, after we were both up for a while, Michael was on the phone and then he just handed it to me. It was Johanna. "I'm sorry about last night. Can I come with you again today? I would like to take some photos, maybe while you paint.

"Of course!" I responded. She told me that she was in another town nearby and that she would come by in a little while. It was Monday and Michael was going to stay at home and work. I offered to crack some macadamia nuts for him since I had heard him say earlier to Johanna that she owed him two buckets of cracked nuts—sort of a payment on her part for all the things he did for her. Later when she arrived, he mentioned that he had heard she was to move. She said that she knew of two other offers she had to house sit, adding though that they weren't available for a couple days.

"Well, you can stay here with me," he said to her. We got ready to leave for the day. "Don't you have to go to the doctor in Hilo?" Michael reminded her.

"I'm going to change it to Wednesday," she said while looking at me.

"Well, you better call now! It's 10 and the appointment is in two hours." I was surprised how much Michael knew about her schedule. She called the doctor, identifying herself using her Indian name, Pune. Smiling at me watching, she changed her appointment. She told Michael when it was for he or someone else would be driving her there. We then left for our excursion of the day.

Once we were driving, I noticed her to be quite tired. She said she spent the night at a friend's and didn't get much sleep. She moved over in the front seat to get next to me and she rested her head on my shoulder. "I'm going to miss you when you're gone," she said softly. "I brought something for you." She reached down and brought out a plastic grocery bag that was filled with leaves that looked like bay leaves. "They're cocoa leaves my friends grow. Have you ever tried them like this?"

"No. I haven't. I haven't even had any coke for about ten years."

"Dis is really mild, like coffee or something. You have to add a little baking soda to draw out the coke." she said as she stuffed my mouth with a handful of leaves. "Juss chew it for a while," she instructed. The taste wasn't nice but after a while my lips became numb like after you snort it. Once it was played, I pulled over to spit it out on the passenger side, leaning over her lap to spit it out the door. She patted me on the back like she was getting a baby to burp. As we drove along we listened repeatedly to a cassette she brought along.

Our long drive brought us around the island to a place I hadn't been to yet. She sat there languid and quiet and I felt her body as I drove. When I stopped she felt my arm or held my hand in her lap, holding my pinky with one hand and my thumb with the other, examining the back of my hand with keen observation. Finally we stopped where the road ended and there was another lookout area that looked out to the ocean and cliffs. I found a place to paint just off the road at the edge of a field. I leaned my larger canvas this time next to a fence and the parked car sheltered me a little from the wind. Johanna watched me paint then she climbed into the car and slept. My painting took about three or more hours and tourists walked by taking pictures or asking if they could take pictures of me painting. Some peered into the front seat of the car and saw the blonde woman curled up in the front seat. After I was done she woke up.

"Where should we go tonight?" I asked her as we drove off.

"Wherever you want."

"Let's find a hotel or something back in Kona," I said to her and we drove the good distance there. We experienced a beautiful sunset of blues and reds from the road perched high on the steep slope in Kona. I noticed a sign: Rainbow B&B, so I turned into the driveway that went down into a lush garden-like setting with a few cabins scattered about. Leaving her in the car, I walked up to the house that displayed where the office was. A German couple ran the place and I rented a cabin that was available, returned to the car a drove the short distance to our cabin. We hadn't eaten all day so I drove out to get us some food while she took a shower. When I returned she was on the couch watching TV, seeming quite worn out and without an appetite for the Chinese food I got for us.

"I like to watch da noose," she said.

"Da noose?" I didn't understand.

"That tells about things going on."

"Oh, the news!" I said and we laughed.

"I don't know why I always say da!" she said with a smile. Reclining on the couch with her head in my lap, she started to doze off. We soon went to bed and I set the alarm for 2AM for I wanted to see that meteor shower. We made love but she wasn't particularly responsive, being tired still, strung out from the night before. The alarm later woke me up, but not her. I nudged her but she wasn't up for going outside. I went outside and looked up for a while only to see a couple shooting stars. Returning inside, I told her there was a hammock outside so she followed me out to it with a blanket wrapped around her body and her head hanging limp; then she lay next to me on her side with her face on my chest. It was nothing spectacular. In ten minutes I saw only a handful of shooting stars all coming from the same direction. She saw none in her continued slumber. We went back in to sleep in the bed.

In the morning she asked me if I could get her some coffee. I walked up to the owner's place and the woman said that breakfast is served up there on their deck so I went back to get Johanna and we both went up to their deck. We walked by a pet Vietnamese pot-bellied pig with a big ring in its nose. There were other exotic pets that they had around the gardens on their property.

"Good morning!" the attractive German hostess said to us. "I didn't know if you were coming back." She ushered us out to where the food was and there were three other couples seated at a table. I got us some fruit and Johanna sat down at the table.

"We're from Minnesota and we're going diving today!" an uppity woman said to us. Johanna just looked at her with a blank expression and it made me sort of laugh.

The hosts had all these caged parrots around their house and on the deck which had a wonderful view of the ocean. Below in little pools were carp. We saw peacocks down there, white ones which Johanna informed me were very rare. Pair by pair the other couples left the table until we were there alone. I put my bare foot on hers and she looked into my eyes and smiled. One of the caged parrots was uttering something and it made her laugh. I didn't understand so I asked her what was so funny.

"He says hello in Finnish!" she told me as her eyes watered like she was about to cry.

"Just for you!" I remarked.

We left in the car to drive back and I dropped her off by her driveway so she could go pack up her stuff for she was to move out of her little shack. I continued up to Michael's to say goodbye for I was leaving that day. I showed him my newest painting and he said, "You make it look so easy. Do you think Johanna has picked up some tips on how to paint while watching you these past days?"

"Well yesterday it took me about three hours and she slept in the car for most of the time." He was a bit flustered but asked me how my stay had been. "Fantastic!" I told him. I thanked him for his hospitality, paid him for the costs of the rented car, and I gave him a small painting I had done earlier back at Oahu. I left his house and went down to where Johanna was. She had packed up one suitcase so far. I sat down and she stood in front of me, put her arms around my neck and held my head to her breast. I could hear her heart beating as she stood there.

"Can't you stay?" she asked me.

"I can't because I can't keep renting a car and I have no way of getting around." I wanted to give her more reasons, but as much as I liked her, I knew that I just couldn't stay therewith her. She seemed to understand.

"We'll be together again in another place," she assured me. "Can we go to the store before you go?"

"Of course!" We went to the closest town and went into a store where she bought a few things then I drove her back. It was our last moments together. I put my hand on her thigh and she clung to my arm. "That was so much fun being with you!" I said in the silence. "You have such a great energy."

"No, I don't really." She started to cry. I stopped at her driveway.

"It's all coming to an end," I said to her.

"Let's not look at it like that." She had cleared up a bit and now seemed quite happy. "An end is always a beginning." We kissed there in the car then she got out. "You'll write me won't you?"

"Yes, but you move around so much! How can I find you?"

"Just send it to Michael." she said and she walked up that grassy road. As I backed my car out she blew kisses at me, smiling beautifully like she was some unearthly angel. I drove back to the airport in Hilo, caught my plane to Honolulu where I later caught my flight to Rarotonga, Cook Islands.

Rarotonga is almost due south of the Hawaiian Islands and it is at about the same latitude but in the Southern Hemisphere. We arrived on the plane at night and once I got my bags in the one room airport I joined a woman who was looking for tenants for her hotel. We went off in her van and I rented a room back at her simple hotel.

The next morning I rented a bicycle and pedaled around the island which was an old volcanic one that wasn't very big-it took me just over half an hour to ride around the one road that circumnavigated it. A sharply pointed green mountain about two thousand feet high was in the center of the island and it tapered down to a flat drier coastal area that had lots of palm trees dotting the shoreline. There weren't many sandy beaches but there was a sandy lagoon with patches of coral within the more distant reef that circled the island about a kilometer out, acting as a breakwater for the protected lagoon. It was hot and humid there, trees were flowering and many of the locals wore them either in leis that were around their necks or as crowns on their heads. Others simply pushed a flower behind their ears. Men did this as well as women. I saw goats, chickens and pigs walking about the cinderblock tin roofed shanties that were common dwellings for the native people. The population there seemed about half Maori and half Caucasian for the island was a territory of New Zealand.

After a couple days I found a better rental in a more lush part of the island, better for painting. The man who owned the cabins was an American from North Adams, Massachusetts. He told me he had retired there and that he leased this land for no foreigners were allowed to buy land there. After I checked in, he noted that I hadn't written anything in his logbook as to how I had found his place. I then did and he proceeded to read it out loud: "I rode by on my bike. I guess that's as good a way as any!" he remarked with a smile. I had a nice small cabin that had a bathroom and I stayed there for the rest of my two week stay, making four paintings there before leaving to my next stop, New Zealand.

Flying into New Zealand, I noticed from my view out the window that the ocean was a wonderful jade green and below on the land was a forest of palm-like fern trees. I was excited, knowing that I surely could get good paintings done in this part of the world. How fantastic it was for me to be able to go so far away in a relatively short period of time, flying there through the air as though I came from the clouds. I felt very lucky! To access a distant land like this was a new thing for us human beings, and for the landscape artists of the past, a dream. It is a deep human trait to want to go, to explore. I could feel my kindred spirits within me rejoicing.

Once at the airport, I followed some others onto a bus that went into Auckland and I randomly chose a hostel or "backpacker" as they term them there. I walked around in the small city which culturally wasn't much unlike my part of the world back in New England, mostly white people with a spattering of Asians and Maoris. It was a pretty place with palm trees and Magnolias in the well planned parks that dotted the hilly terrain that overlooked the ocean in almost all directions. I was relieved when I went to an ATM machine and was able to withdraw money from my savings account in Rockland. It gave me New Zealand dollars which was weak against the US dollar, rendering my money a doubled value.

I decided to do a little trip that went up north of Auckland. I was heading to Brisbane, Australia to visit my sister Dinah and her family in two weeks, so on the interim I got a package that went north to Pahia by bus, then a plane to Great Barrier Island, then back by plane to the Coromandel Peninsula, then a bus back to Auckland all for $120.

My first leg to Pahia was nice. I enjoyed the four hour bus ride there, seeing the countryside, the birds and plants that were all new to me. It is always fascinating to see the manifestations of nature out there in different lands. We headed north but it was toward the equator, toward the warmer more tropical locales. It was an odd experience for me as a Northern Hemisphere person to know that it was the month of December, but to feel the June-like sunshine and experience the longest days of the year. Pahia is a town in an area known as the Bay of Islands. The ocean was rich with marine life: penguins, dolphins, tuna, and sharks. I did one painting out on an island that I took a ferry to, and another right in the town near my hotel rental. I was able to paint, capturing the jade green color of the ocean which had purplish shadows cast down onto it from the partly cloudy skies.

My next destination was Great Barrier Island, an island about forty miles offshore. I caught a six-seater plane that bounced a bit in turbulents, but it was scenic. Approaching the island, I saw its small mountains and undeveloped land with lots of trees and broad white sand beaches along the coast. Our plane was the only one at the small air strip. I joined the others in a van that took us to the little town which was just a scattering of a few houses and a store or two. There, I found a cheap room.

The island was an interesting place. I saw strange plants like the gooseberries that were fruiting this time of year. There were these brown parrots that ate the berries which I gathered were fermenting, making the parrots drunk and rather boisterous. I saw an evergreen that had a purple flower and the exotic Tui, a black songbird with a marvelous white necklace and crown. The island wasn't very populated. I rented a bike, pedaled around in some rainy weather. I left by plane after three days, unable to get a painting in there.

At the Coromandel peninsula, I experienced another fine place and there I rented by a beach, a hotel room with a kitchenette. I made a painting from the beach which was covered with orange and white striped clamshells known there as pipis. Strange limestone pillars dotted the horizon out in the green ocean and in front of me on the beach, black oystercatchers with red legs sifted through the sand with their long beaks; and gangs of gulls, also with red legs, stole their catch if they could. There was a significant tide there and as the tide became high, the water became disturbed from the short rolling waves, churning up the light brown sand to make the inland water appear yellowish brown. After painting on the spot, I bring them home to my hotel room to finish them up. Once they're dry, I take them off the stretchers and roll them up. In this town I sent a couple tubes of completed paintings back to New York to my sister Susan's.

After painting, I walked around, along the beach and through the town. I was very much alone and I longed to find a woman but I didn't meet any there. I did see one beautiful girl in this town. I saw her in a store window as I walked by, so

I sat on a wall there for a while to watch her from a distance. She was dark, like an Indian, a Maori woman in her mid twenties. Often the Maori girls were a bit heavy, but this one had a perfect figure. She wore a sarong wrapped around her wide hips and a green shirt that hugged her thin waist and exposed her nice chest. I went into the shop where she worked just so I could see her more closely. She had an Indian bindi stuck to the middle of her forehead and her black hair fanned away from the symmetry of her beautiful face. I looked around pretending I was shopping even though most of the stuff there was for girls. I was lucky enough to see her smile at me, but I was too shy to say anything to her. I did see her a day later at the supermarket and she was with her boyfriend, a lucky blonde fellow.

I had to head back to Auckland by bus for it was time to fly to Brisbane. I called my sister Dinah to let her know when I was arriving. "It'll be nice to see you, but you can't stay here!" she said to me, warding off the fact that I was coming.

"I won't stay with you all very long." I said back, wondering why it was that she had earlier pressed that I should come visit them. It wasn't something unusual for me to experience a type of alienation from my sisters, but it never made it seem alright. "I want to explore the vicinity and go paint." She agreed to come pick me up at the airport at Brisbane, about an hour's drive from where they lived in Surfer's Paradise.

Once off the plane, I found Dinah waiting at the gate and we went to her van to drive back to their house. She told me that she had been back to Santa Barbara to see Dad and that it didn't look good for him. He had been on chemo therapy for almost a year and they decided to stop the treatment, meaning he would die soon. We were driving to the left, as is done in Australia, but she was traveling in the right lane on the highway. A few faster cars came up behind us, paused for her to move over then passed us to our left. I told her to move over to the left lane unless she was passing. She angrily told me that it was really aggravating to have someone tell her how to drive: but consequently, she did move her van over to the other lane. Their house and car were supplied by her husband Whip's acting job. This area of Australia had a Disney studio and he was doing forty or so episodes of a series, Flipper, a remake of the old show with the dolphin. The dolphin wasn't in the show all that much, and it wasn't as good as the original Flipper, but it gave Whip a good paying job as an actor and it gave the family a chance to see a different part of the world.

We got to their house, one of those newly built suburban neighborhoods where all the houses look the same. They had a pool and an Astroturf tennis court there at their house. Their two daughters, Molly and Ella, were going to grade school and had picked up Aussie accents. They also had a two-year-old son, Ben. A nanny was there much of the time for help. I spent the night at their house then left the next day by bus for Byron Bay for I felt that I was crowding them with my imposing visit. I told Dinah that I would be back in five days to spend Christmas with them.

Byron Bay was nice with its long white beaches and pristine ocean that had ideal rolling waves for surfing. Johanna had lived there and had suggested that I go there for it had a lot of young people. Her son was born there. When I got off the bus I looked for a place rent but there were no vacancies, due to Christmas holiday season. I walked through the little town carrying my seabag and canvas golfbag that held my stretchers and canvas. I finally found a room but it was at one of the most expensive hotels there, costing me over a hundred dollars for one night. I certainly didn't want to pay that much but sometimes this unplanned, open-ended way of traveling had its costs. Besides, all the money I had earned went towards food and shelter and some art supplies.

I woke up early the next morning in Byron, looking for a place to paint. I walked along the beach and noticed dolphins swimming close to shore. An early surfer noticed them too and he sat up on his board, floating and watching them as they scooted by him underwater. Continuing on to the end of the beach, I found a lookout tower with a platform up high for viewing the panorama so I returned later there to paint. I went and got my paints and a large rectangular canvas. Leaning it against the fence that went around the deck, I painted while kneeling on my shins on a towel I brought with me.

The morning went by and soon I had many onlookers. It was a Saturday and Christmas was in a few days so it was crowded at the beach with vacationers. I didn't like to have people looking over my shoulder as I painted, but sometimes it's something that you have to deal with. One woman asked me what I was doing. I gestured to the view of the bay in front of us and said, "I'm painting."

"My mother paints too! I'm from Sidney. I just got married and we're on our honeymoon—brought the dog and everything!" I stopped painting to look back at her. She was a blonde beauty. Her hair was cut short just to her shoulders exposing her thin neck. She had a beautiful body and was in a bikini top with shorts. Looming over my back she tugged on the leash of her little dog. "Where are you from?"

"I'm from the United States," I told her as I went back to moving the brush over the canvas. She watched a bit more, asking me more questions like she wanted to get to know me. She left after a while, back to her groom I suppose.

After about three hours, I completed my painting and carried it back through the throng that had amassed on the beach. Some women sunbathed topless for nudity was accepted there. I brought the painting back to my room where I neatly kept working on it. I found a cheaper hotel room but it rained for the next few days so I didn't get another painting done.

I nicely had a place right next to two Australian Greek women. They invited me into their room for cocktails so I joined them even though I didn't drink. They were party girls and they kept talking on their cell phones in Greek. There was, I noticed, quite a large contingent of Greek immigrants there in Australia. There was even a Greek speaking channel on the TV. I liked Byron Bay but I headed back to Dinah's for Christmas Eve.

Their new plans were to go back to California for a week the day after Christmas. We all went to church at dusk on Christmas Eve to a very casual Mass. Christmas carols were sung but the Aussies weren't all that familiar with them so the words to the songs were beamed onto a screen behind the altar. As we left the church we saw the magnificent and eerie sight of thousands of fruit bats the size of crows flying overhead towards the forests in the inland hills.

We went back to their house and I helped Dinah wrap some presents for their kids. Once it got late she brought out a joint. She always had been a drinker and smoker and enjoyed the relief from built up tensions of the day, becoming noticeably happier once she has a few drinks of wine in her. We talked a little while sitting outside in the hot summer night. A cacophony of quacks came from duck frogs in a pond nearby.

"Whip!" she called out for her husband. "That's all I ask that he be able to just sit down like this for a while and relax with me!" He was off in the kitchen cleaning things.

The next day was Christmas and the girls fervently opened their presents, the way hungry dogs riffle through trash bags to get at what's inside. I admit that I had been like that too as a child. We all used to wait at the bottom of the stairs, peering into the living room to see the booty of presents for all six of us. Once Mom and Dad woke up and came downstairs we had the green light to find what was ours.

It was learned that day at Dinah's that there was no Santa. Ella figured it out by comparing the wrapping paper used by Santa to the wrapping paper she had seen around the house. "There's no Santa." she said with a clever smile. Molly, the older one, had a harder time with it and she started to cry.

"You lied to me!" she stated to both her parents. They consoled her by saying that he is an imaginary person but very much alive.

"He's like the tooth fairy," I butted in. "You don't believe in them right?"
"Yes I do," Molly said with a smile.
"Uncle Sam…don't blow it!" their dad boomed out loudly with sarcasm.

Later that morning they all packed up to leave on their trip back to the States. They had planned to have some friends stay at their house while they were gone and offered that I could stay there too if I wanted. I wanted to explore more so I declined their offer and kept exploring around.

Dinah had bought me a present that was a group trip to Frazier Island, a large barrier island just north of Brisbane. I told her I didn't want to do it and she got a little angry. "You can't cash it in Sam!" she told me thinking that's my incentive for not wanting to do it.

"No, I don't want to cash it in!"

"You're just getting the heebie jeebies because you're going to be stuck with all those people for three days!"

"Yeah, you're right!" I was not interested in going on a bus with a bunch of tourists. She knew this too. Her present was somewhat suspect in its implication. Spitefully, I went on this trip to Frazier Island.

I was unable to paint on this excursion since I was on a tour bus, but I did see some interesting things. The island, a short ferry ride from the mainland, is the largest sand island in the world. There were some forests on the island, though most of it was sand dunes, and the little streams that ran under the trees had brilliant white sand riverbeds. Rain pours much of the year there accounting for the spring we visited that gushed cool water out a ways up a hill, creating a natural waterslide that was crowded with visitors on this extremely hot day. Our guide in the bus suggested that we not go swimming in the ocean for danger of sharks and poisonous jellyfish. We drove in the bus along the wide flat beach that stretched a hundred kilometers in a straight line. I noticed people dragging pieces of meat tied to a string along the sand near the waterline. I learned this was bait for bloodworms which poked their heads through the sand and were consequently yanked out at over a meter long! I spent two nights there, having my own room in a dormitory type building, like the whole thing was some fieldtrip for schoolgoers. At last this excursion was over and I headed by bus back to Dinah's house.

It was New Year's Eve and her Aussie friends who were staying at their house invited me to go into town with them. I went for a little while but there was such heavy drinking and flat out boredom that I went back to the house. It seemed that in Australia there were many compulsive drinkers or alcoholics. I had come to see drinking and drunkenness as complete idiot's delight so I bypassed the observations of that evening's folly. I spent the night at Dinah's and then the next day I headed back to Byron Bay which I preferred more. I found a cheaper room there to rent and I frequented the beach, body surfing in the ocean and carousing with the chicks on the beach. I did another painting set up right on the beach but experienced more rainy days.

With ten more days to go before I left Australia, I headed back to Dinah's with hopes that I could stay there for I was spending too much money on rentals nor had I seen much of them. They had just returned from their long trip back to the States and traveling had stirred things up so it wasn't exactly a good place for me to be. The reports of Dad were grim—he was on his last legs and could die at any time. At night Dinah and I were talking out their patio and she mentioned that he was going to be cremated. For some reason she mentioned that Mom had been cremated with her wedding ring still on.

"Really, I didn't know that!"

"Too bad, you could have hawked it!" she said to me with an angry face, alluding back to my pre-Navy actions of selling the stolen silver.

"I would be the last one to get that!" I replied, inferring how she and the others got all sorts of things that I didn't.

"You have a real chip on your shoulder, don't you!" she said with an angry expression, resembling an animal that was about to bite. Whip, hearing the start of a fight, came out and told Dinah to stop and to relax. He then turned toward me and gave me a strange look as though I was an intruder or something—I realized then that I was just that. I told them that I would find somewhere else to stay for the rest of my time there.

I found a flat the next day in Surfer's Paradise. It was up in one of the high rise buildings that bordered the beach, the paradise for surfers. I hung out there until my plane ticket's departure date. I left Australia having spent well over $2,000. I only did two paintings there in my month's stay. I headed back to New Zealand, changing my planned flight to Papayette, Tahiti. I wanted to explore more of that country for it had great scenes to paint, the weather was just right, and the dollar went a long way there.

Once back in Auckland, I bought myself a ticket that went to the South Island, giving me three stops at places on New Zealand's larger but less populated island. My first stop was Dunnedin, the Otago region on the southeast coast. The area was experiencing a drought so the rolling grassy hills were parched and brown. I found myself a little motel next to the coast which had sand dunes and cliffs that dropped down to a wavy blue ocean. I was at the same latitude in the southern hemisphere as Maine only it was warmer here all year around due to the warmer ocean currents. I saw large rose bushes and fuchsia shrubs that grew in people's yards. The ocean was rich with birdlife and large seals, so called: sea elephants. The ocean there was rather chilly but not quite as cold as Maine's.

I walked a lot, walking to where I painted and to where I got my food. I frequented a little eatery run by people from Malaysia. They were all smiles to their customers and they served a nice inexpensive plate of fried rice and vegetables. I didn't have any cooking facilities at my room but I went to the big supermarket to get fruit and drinks, savoring their black current juice that was unavailable back in the States. I was fascinated to see that it was alright to go into these big stores barefoot!

Next, I took a shuttle van west across the island to Queenstown. This town was in a mountainous area just inland on a lake. It reminded me of Taos for evergreens grew along the slopes of the mountains. The town's revenue came from tourism, particularly during their winter months for there was a ski resort nearby on mountains known as, The Remarkables. I did a painting of them from the lakeside. There were quite a few young people there for there was a college of some sort in the town. I stayed in Queenstown for five days then took the next leg of my trip by plane to Christchurch.

Once again I showed up there with no planned agenda. I took a bus into this larger city and found a cheap room to rent for a while. They had a piano in their lobby and I played it. My ability to play was rather new but it seemed to have grown on its own. My fingers touched the keys and moved like knew where to go. The music touched a deep sadness inside of me, causing me to cry to myself as I played.

I walked a lot there. "Walking solves all problems" said the Romans. It was a spread out city, "The garden City" for it had many parks and an arboretum with shallow streams where one could see large rainbow trout wriggling about. At the city square there were venders selling crafts and foods. I bought a few jade rings to give later as gifts for they were under ten dollars each. I walked by a big church…the Christ Church? I came across a casino and went in to play Blackjack, winning at first then returning other times only to lose more of my money. This foolishness of gambling interfered with my vague attempts to make a painting there. After a while I flew back to Auckland to explore more of the North Island.

Once there, I took a bus to Rotorura. Back at Rarotonga I had met a Maori man about my age and he had recommended that I go to this place for it was a center for the Maori culture and most of the people who lived there were Maori. Coming into the town on the bus it smelled like a rotten egg. I saw this yellow foam on the lake and thought it to be some industrial pollution. It was sulfur coughed up out of the earth due to the volcanic activity in the area. In the town I noticed that there was a great deal of steam coming out of the ground at various places. Cracks in the sidewalks puffed out steam and sulfur caked around these fissures like it was an orange-yellow frosting. Around many of the houses were stacks that were installed as relief vents for the pressure that came up from beneath. I saw footage on the television in my hotel room of Maoris cooking chickens and corn placed in baskets and lowered into hot steam crevasses. On the same show they alluded to a time in the past when the heads of intruding European invaders were cooked this same way.

The white settlers did the same thing in New Zealand that they did in other areas of the world that they "discovered". There had been a war in the mid 1800's only the white people lost at first to the fierce and strong Maori men; consequently reinforcements came in with more firepower to decimate the local population, much like they had done in the Americas.

I personally felt a type of guilt, belonging to this race of white people, for our foolish antics around the world had caused such intense disturbances. These notions of superiority, property possession, and lack of respect for the other types of people that they came across, were still in fashion in many ways in the culture that I was born into. Knowing these traits to be a portrayal of an inferior type of race, rather than a superior one, I had for much of my life wished that I wasn't a white person. I stayed in this town just a couple days then continued on the bus to New Plymouth, the so called Taranaki region.

New Plymouth was nice, a small city on the western coast with a pointed dormant volcano overlooking the town. I had seen this volcano poking through the clouds when I was flying back from my trip to the South Island and I wanted to go see it and paint it. I found a very cheap "backpacker" there and rented a single room, going off in the daytime to different places to make paintings.

One day after painting I took a walk through this parked and I came across a bird I had never seen, the New Zealand Pigeon. It was a handsome, large bird with colorful blue, gray and green feathers. As I stopped to admire it, it noticed me but didn't fly away. I walked silently closer to it and it tilted its head and looked at me with a magical aura, like it was someone very familiar, puzzled or concerned.

Later that day, I called back to my dad's house in Santa Barbara and learned that he had just died, like five minutes ago. There was to be a family get together soon in Santa Barbara. I went back to Auckland and changed my ticket so I could fly back to the States sooner.

6

Dad's Ashes

I made my way back to Santa Barbara and met up with the others. We all stayed at a hotel that had little cabins as rental units. This, apparently, was the place where the girls stayed when they made visits to Dad and Wendy during holidays. I stayed in a two bedroom cabin, sharing a room with Susan. Dinah, Whip and George slept in the other room. Carrie and her family were in the cabin next door. Eliza and her fiancé stayed at some other hotel and Chris and his family stayed at Wendy's.

It was at this time that we all learned that we had inherited something from Dad. The house at North Haven was given to us all with Dinah named as the trustee. The rest of his estate was bequeathed to Wendy. We also learned that there was a trust fund set up by our grandmother, Ma. It had been initiated in the 1950's with $70,000 and had been invested in very conservative stocks, but was now worth a whopping 1.8 million! Since Dad was one of three children, one third of this money would eventually be divided up amongst us seven; but not until both of his siblings, Henry and Ellen had died. Meanwhile, we would be getting a quarterly dividend check that Dad had been getting all along. There was a check there written out to me for $350.

The next morning we all went in several cars to a place in the low mountains inland to scatter some of Daddy's ashes. It was a cold and overcast New England type of day. A bunch of their elderly friends came along as well, but it was only the relatives who went off a little ways to toss the ashes into the breeze. It was a poorly orchestrated event, almost business-like with nothing very sentimental taking place. The plan was to have a picnic out there but the raw weather wasn't permitting; so we all went to a nearby hotel, rented a convention room and had our picnic in there.

That evening we had a meeting back at the hotel cabin about our house on North Haven and it turned out to be an ugly affair. With a vote there was a majority decision to have Carrie's husband, Jibs, be the moderator. He had recently become the CEO of an internet search engine, Excite.com, company due to his superior management skills. It was mentioned that he brought his sporting tennis game into his profession by bringing tennis balls into his meetings and throwing them at dozing slouchers. Dinah was unhappy that Jibs had been chosen to run the meeting for she felt that it was her responsibility to do it, since Dad had chosen her to be the trustee. Jibs made some rules and the meeting got underway.

It started by figuring out how the house should be run, either communally, or divided into separate portions of ownership. We went around the room so that each person could make a statement that reflected their view. I started by saying that it should stay fully communal. Dinah felt the same way. Then Carrie said that she thought that way at first, but now thought that things would be better taken care of if it was divided up. Susan sat there quietly for it was her turn to speak. She passed as did Eliza, who was next. It was Chris's turn and he too was a proponent of separate ownership. He stated that unless you already have owned a house, you really don't know what sort of things go into managing it. His entire statement seemed to be addressed to me for he was looking at me the entire time he spoke. George too was obviously in with having his own separate spot within the house.

"All those in favor of separate ownership, raise your hand," Jibs said to the group of brothers and sisters seated in the room. Dinah and I needed Susan and Eliza's vote. With Carrie, George and Chris raising their hand up, Susan waited and then slowly raised hers. Eliza, delaying to see what Susan did, then raised hers as well. Both Dinah and I are displeased that they all want to do it this way. I was not particularly surprised by their decisions for I recognized that it was most common amongst the rich to divide things, not understanding the precepts of true unity for their world is divided, a multiplicity of separate things. Dinah and I are the only ones who had inherited our mother's egalitarian side. Dinah was quite angry with them and she started to voice her dismay. Jibs cut her off, saying with a sharp turn of his head, "You've had your point heard!" Dinah, startled by his aggressive refereeing, groped for words. The other naysayers laughed at her defeat.

"Why is everybody laughing at me?" she said frowning and then she began to cry. Jibs' competitive stance quickly melted and the others just watched her sob with her head bent over into her lap. She then resurrected herself and said, "I'm crying because Dad's dead…at least I have some emotions!"

"That's not fair!" Eliza spurted.

"This whole thing has been like some sort of business deal or something! What's wrong with you people?" Dinah said in a loud voice, then went back into her recline.

"I'm going back over to my family!" Carrie said and she got up from her chair and made a swift exit. Her husband smartly got up too and followed her out, almost like he was carrying his queen's coattails.

The meeting broke up. There were more discussions out on the porch but it only added to the tensions that had been generated. It was truly bizarre how we couldn't really cope with each other when we all got together, as rare as it was. We had come together to pay homage to our deceased father, to mourn his loss, yet there was no crying or waves of sadness that we all had experienced when our mother had died. On the contrary, what was revealed were the uglier aspects of what our father had extended into us—this poverty of the rich that I have talked about, being spread into the world like a brush fire that burns up everything in its path.

From Los Angeles, I bought a one-way ticket to Boston and I made my way back up to Maine, catching a bus to Rockland to take the ferry out to North Haven. Like the year before, I was there way too early. I had to rough it again. The gray ocean of the Penobscot Bay during the dormant winter season was a sharp contrast to the vibrant greenish blue ocean of the Tasman Sea halfway around the world. There were zero lobster pots which later in the summer dot the surface of the water like floating candies of different bright colors. It was quite cold in the house and I found my warmer clothes and dressed in layers.

The first morning I was awakened by a loud crash downstairs. It sounded as though someone had thrown some heavy boards onto the deck. I hopped up out of bed and went down below to see what had happened. Strangely, the top shelf of a cabinet loaded with electrical and plumbing items had come cascading down to the workshop floor, scattering little items all over the place. I was stunned for this loud noise had coincided with the dream I had just had.

In the dream I was sitting at a small round table with these two thugs. They were in sort of preppy attire, Brooks Brothers' shirts and things, but they had ugly scarred faces. In the dream, I laughed nervously but their faces remained grim; then suddenly, the bigger of the two slammed his fist down onto the table. This loud crash coincided with the noise that woke me up. It was to me an almost comical wake up call from my father, who never let us sleep past 9 AM.

I did my usual thing: I painted pictures that I knew I could sell later that summer. I played my keyboard and watched some television at night. Having moved around so much the six months prior, I kept traveling in my dreams, going to places that I had never even been to yet! I had to pace myself through the weeks of cold weather and the hardships of having no running water. I smoked up a jar of marijuana leaves I had from the previous year's crop. It didn't do much but give me a cough. By mid May the water was turned on and I was able to take a hot bath.

Every experience that we have is relative to our other experiences and knowing this one can minimize one's suffering. We can even creatively accentuate blissful moments that might not normally occur. My hot bath, after weeks of its absence, made it a sublime experience. If you fast for a couple days food becomes more than tasty when you get to eat it. If you've lost your freedom, you become ecstatic when set free. The status of being free isn't noticed the same way unless it has been lost. The contrasting elements of experience such as happiness and despair are mutually related, creating each other. There is up because there is down, darkness because there's light, love because of hate, and life because of death. There is no you, unless there is me!

This simple wisdom is widely lacking in our culture today due to our materialistic nature. Many people in our rich country are very unhappy and they have almost no reason to be so, in comparison to what others go through in the destitute places around the world. With so much going for themselves, they are lost, separate entities in a world of separate things. They go to doctors to get pills to sedate their self-made illnesses to eliminate their despair for a while; or they get drunk to check out for a while, thinking this will ease their pain. My father had once said to me, "Nobody's happy doing anything they do. If they say they are, they're lying!" This poor man was hopefully set free upon his death.

Late that May, I had an enlightening experience. On a clear afternoon I went for a walk up a nearby hill, the highest spot on the island. Spring comes late to an island off the cold Maine coast so the plants and trees were just coming out, all was fresh and new. A path led me up through birches and spruce to the rocky summit where I surveyed the expansive views of the ocean and other islands. It was a little chilly up there, so I retreated back down the path to a warmer sheltered area in the sun. I squatted down next to the ground and noticed the ferns growing everywhere. A little one about a foot tall was next to my left knee. Looking at it, I thought of the huge fern trees I had seen back in New Zealand halfway around the world. Ferns are such a prolific and ancient species. I studied its body-like form which seemed to unfurl itself as I examined it. I softly touched it with the back of my fingers and I said to it in a whisper, "Aren't you lovely!" I felt a tingling run through my body like it had cast a spell on me, communicating a deep but subtle message of its love.

It wasn't until later that July that some of my siblings came up to Maine. Susan came up from New York with her latest boyfriend, another successful writer. I showed them an arrowhead I had recently found out at Burnt Island. She was incredulous that I had found it, thinking that it was something that I had purchased somewhere and pretended to have found it. I have found about a dozen or so of them in my life and she none, so it was understandable that she was such a skeptic. I also showed them something I had written, inspired by my experience with that fern. Susan denied its authenticity as well, claiming that it was something that Robert Frost had written. Her boyfriend, Walter, laughed at her, and sympathetically confided that it wasn't.

In early August all of the others showed up for we were going to have a service for our father. Once everyone was there, we had another meeting about the house. A change of heart had taken place with Susan and Eliza about how to manage the house. They were now with me and Dinah, so we had a majority decision to keep mutual ownership and to keep the house undivided. There was still a great deal of tension between us and a bit of an argument about what had happened back at the other meeting in Santa Barbara. Jibs was there but not participating this time. He strolled around between rooms in the house as Dinah orchestrated things this time.

The next morning we all went off to scatter the rest of Dad's ashes. We wanted to scatter them in the same place we had scattered Mum's, in a cove just around the bend in the Fox Island Thorofare, but it was very windy making it way too difficult to go off in little boats, so we went by land.

The cove was accessible just off the golf course so Wendy, Dad's brother and sister, and the seven of his children and their families all met there at a certain time in the morning. We walked across the busy course to the waterhole. I led them there for I knew where to go. "Are you sure you know where you're going?" Susan said to me with a puckered look on her face. I assured her that I did and I beckoned for the throng to come for they delayed the play of many confused golfers.

We made it down to the waterhole, a scenic par three. It was dead low tide and we made our way out onto the rocks, finding a perfect place at the end of a point where there was a little rock platform where each person could stand to say something before tossing the ashes into the stiff breeze.

We gathered together in silence and Dinah's daughter Ella started. She hopped up on the flat stone and read a poem she had written about her grandfather. "He liked making boats, carving ducks, and he always ate some food off my plate at dinner." She went on to say more things that she was familiar with about

Dad. Chris was the bearer of the baggie filled with ashes and he stood next to the pulpit rock, giving her access to a handful of ashes once she had finished.

Molly, Dinah's eldest, was next. "Goodbye Grandpa!" she said as tears rolled down her cheek. She threw some wildflowers she had up into the air and the wind carried them off onto the brown seaweed that carpeted the rocky low tide zone. A handful of ashes followed. The silence of everyone listening and the whispering of the strong breeze that blew through us kicked up an upwelling of emotions inside of me and I began to cry. It wasn't a sad thing really that I felt, but a feeling of great joy of a life that extended through all of us that were there. By seeing my niece cry, I felt a bonding that identified me with her and all of them there.

When my turn came up, I gained my composure and said, "Thank you for game six of the 1975 World Series!" This was the game that Carlton Fisk hit the famous tying homerun that he urged to stay fair while he straddle the first base line.

"We'll miss you George," said his sister.

"Goodbye Mr. Minot!" said Chris's wife Fanny, sparking a little laughter, for Dad strangely didn't allow his children's spouses call him by his first name. More gave their thanks and regards like it was their last farewell to him somewhere there amongst us. Lastly, Eliza stood up on the rock and said nothing. Looking partially up to the sky with a stoic face, she launched her flowers and then the last of the ashes up into the air where they floated down to the pile of flowers and the last physical remnants of our father.

We gave each other hugs and people cried together. At last, the separateness that was so common between us disappeared, vaporized by the love we all had for Dad. Any animosities that we had toward each other were gone and insignificant, creating the wonderful experience of a large, loving family that is one.

0-595-31642-5